DEDICATION

This book is dedicated to those brave souls who are about to
break out of their shells of conformity and change their lives
forever!

Hire-Education For Job Seekers

Twelve Easy Steps To Get Hired

GARY and WENDY SWANSON

CONTENTS

INTRODUCTION

The *scattergun* approach to job hunting, where you go from one company to the next, filling out applications and leaving resumes, is of little use unless you teach your resume how to talk!

People hire *people*! Now before you begin printing your protest signs and gather a group, we know that lots of companies want to see your resume up front and applications by mail in advance, but we are mainly concerned at the point where you get your first chance at human contact!

Knowing full well that you must get your *foot in the door*, before anything real is apt to begin; it is the eyeball to eyeball moment that I want to primarily deal with. That one-on-one time where you meet in the arena and you no longer can hide behind your anonymity. You are now on stage! Fully exposed in your first performance, and depending on how you deliver your lines, and how your audience reacts, will determine whether the curtain will open on act 2!

Our job is to assist you to get **your job!**

So you've just beaten yourself up for weeks and months just trying to get a job!

You've gone from trying to get that job you really wanted to being ready to accept most anything that will pay enough to keep you alive so you can keep searching for a better choice.

Believe it or not, networking may be the best way to find a new job. We all have friends, relatives, acquaintances, and former colleagues. Reaching out to these people and just having a normal, everyday conversation with them can clue you into job positions that may not be advertised or will be coming open shortly.

No, it's not being pushy or taking advantage of anyone if you have already developed a good rapport with them. If you have an agreeable relationship with someone, where there has already been some give and take; perhaps you've helped them out with a problem or given them good advice in the past, why not discuss with them the fact you are looking for work?

People like doing business with people they already know and like, and the same is true of employers. Maybe your cousin Joe has a job he likes at a great company, and he's doing well there; he likes them and they like Joe. Well Joe just might know of an opening that is coming up at his company, and he can tell you the best way to go about applying there for a job; from who to talk to, to what the requirements of the position are, and to some insight into the person you could be working for. In addition, he can also serve as a reference.

Start reaching out to those people you already know. Don't forget about casual acquaintances like someone from the gym you go to, or from the church you attend, even your doctor or dentist.

Perhaps you are a member of a civic organization or club, a historic society, or a non-profit group? Talk to those people as well.

If you are not a part of any organization, join one that you share an interest with and start making connections. There are tons of non-profits out there that would welcome your help. Their members are from many walks of life and you never know who you might come in contact with. Besides, you'll be doing something to give back to your community and it will look terrific on your resume!

Bet on yourself — If you're reading this book, you already have shown that you have what it takes to succeed. Losers go from business to business, filling out applications and hoping for a job angel to drop down from employment heaven and give them a job.

What do they get instead; a big black rejection raven who poops on their hat!

Winners select where they want to work, and home in on this goal, and they make it happen!

Now that we have licked our wounds enough, let's spend the time to totally change what we've been doing and go back all the way to the basics.

Yes, the very things that we sometimes ignore, because we've gone beyond that stage, right? Well, let us welcome you back to the basics of *hire* education.

GARY and WENDY SWANSON

1 THE PROCESS FROM THE EMPLOYER'S VIEWPOINT

First of all, let's talk about the process of finding a job from the other side of the desk. Don't be one of those visual vultures who spend their time searching hour after hour, day after day, waiting for the ideal job to appear so they can swoop down and land on a meal ticket!

Ain't gonna happen! Why would it?

Put yourself in the employer's seat: Let's say you have a good paying position coming up that you know people will be lining up to get. Do you really want to put yourself, or your management, through the agony of interviewing maybe hundreds of applicants, one after the other? No, of course not! You will likely call a *head hunter;* an employment company that will screen these people for you.

Yes, that's absolutely correct — The employer will pay a fee, and depending on the level of expertise required and the salary involved, it can amount to a huge amount of expense!

Now, you ask; "Why would a company pay another company when they can just run an ad and get hundreds of applicants?" Simple; there are numerous reasons. First of all, the company may be planning to discharge a person in their employ for poor performance, or they may have plans to promote a current worker, and they don't want to start a stampede of internal turmoil by making it known. You ask, "Why would the company not want to give their employees a chance?"

Maybe no one in their current employ is qualified, or maybe the only person qualified is so valuable where they are currently at, that the company cannot afford to lose them in their present capacity. They feel they must hire someone over them, even though it may be necessary to increase their current compensation just to keep them where they are. Rather than shaking their entire company up by having a flood of internal requests, and then a huge attitude problem by turning down those who apply and whom they reject, they can take their time with no one being the wiser.

Then, when they have confidentially interviewed the candidates sent by the head hunter, they make a decision, and when the person being promoted receives the news, the replacement comes on board. Although there will certainly be some hurt feelings, no current employees will feel the same level of resentment that they would have, had they interviewed for the position and then were turned down.

Most always, this transition, if made properly, will leave everyone feeling that the new arrival must have much more experience than they, and disruption is minimal. This also gives the employer a chance to talk individually to those people who may have hurt feelings and sooth any *ruffled feathers*.

Even if the job opening is not that high a paying position, most companies are not adequately equipped with staff to interview hordes of applicants. In today's job market, this process will prevent an employer from being deluged with applicants.

Some employers advertise a position and require applications and resumes in advance, so now it comes down to who can write a flowery enough resume and neatly fill out an application, and be at the mercy of your past experience, which may not be enough. There lies the disadvantage you have as a job seeker!

You may very well be the perfect fit for the job advertised, but unless you can somehow attract the employer's attention, you may never even get to the interview.

Truth be known, most people are very poor at selling themselves! Whether due to fear of being braggadocios, or maybe people just don't see their good points enough to make an adequate pitch in order to point out the benefits in hiring them!

This is why employment agencies thrive.

GARY and WENDY SWANSON

2 HEAD HUNTERS

My first job after my military hitch was up, was selling door to door. I had no idea of what I wanted to do for a living, so this was an easy way to pay my bills until I decided on a career. I did this job for over a year, and still hadn't a clue of what I wanted to do. I only really knew that having my nose flattened by slamming doors had a demoralizing effect on me! So, I began perusing the help wanted ads in the newspaper.

In order that the reader may fully understand the importance of the entire process of seeking employment, we need to take a complete look at the inside secrets of just one employment firm.

I came across an ad for an employment counselor with a famous national employment agency. Although I had never used a firm like this, I envisioned a cushy desk job, no more wear and tear on my car or my shoes, and learning a prestigious career.

What I got was a commissioned position selling people! At least it was inside work and I had an office!

My first day I was led to a huge metal cabinet that was filled with probably a hundred boxes of business cards. Each box of cards had a different name preprinted. All the names were simple and short. The manager said, "Who do you want to be? Pick your alias!" So I chose my new identity, and from that day on I was "Joe Lee." I soon met Bill Brown, Cathy Green, Ron Jones, and an office full of easily pronounced names that worked well in newspaper ads and the human memory.

We only knew each other by our chosen names, and were not allowed to reveal our true identities to each other or anyone else connected with our company. We became actors the minute we came to work each day, and stayed *in character* until we left at night.

I quickly learned the job and was shocked to learn that we *did not* have most of the employment positions that we advertised! The shock was quickly overcome with a well-practiced presentation. By the end of my first day, I had become indoctrinated to the *con*! I call it the con, because it really was a con game, but one that had an actual benefit to our applicants and of course to us!

I was soon advertising fake jobs, asking people to call my fake name, and I was becoming known as the man to see for your next job!

Now don't get me wrong, the job I did made a lot of people happy. Even six months after I left this company, I was stopped at a traffic light and I heard, "Mr. Lee, Mr. Lee!" and a man ran across three lanes of traffic to reach in my car to shake my hand and thank me profusely for the job I got him! He said, "This is the best job I ever had, and I owe it all to you!" All I did was take a talented individual, learn all about him, and then sell him to a company that I chose for him.

What I did for him, he would not have been able to do for himself, so we both had a benefit.

You probably wonder by now, "How can someone with a phony name, advertising a job that does not exist, help anyone?"

Here is the entire secret to this system, and perhaps a major key to understanding human behavior. You may even learn something about your own persona!

A great percentage of the American job force goes through the monotonous day to day repetition of a robot-like existence, and at any given time, their frustration level can easily be triggered to look for a new job!

Sometimes the better job one does, the more they are ignored by their superiors. Why? The old, *squeaky wheel gets the grease* theory. We all know people who repeat each *Groundhog Day* with professional and well-practiced skill. Very likely, although appreciated by their employers, they are the ones most apt to be ignored! Even though it seems like the ideal situation, people for the most part are gregarious and need to feel appreciated. Being taken for granted is a very common problem and a major reason behind seemingly happy employees suddenly resigning with no prior indication of dissatisfaction with their jobs.

Callous employers or just the more normal complacent attitude toward someone who doesn't make any waves is a big reason for these superior people to look elsewhere for employment. This happens a lot more than most statistics ever indicate. In many cases an employer may purposely underplay a staff member's accomplishments because of a fear that paying your worker's compliments on their performance may precipitate in them a feeling of being worth more money! This way, to keep an employee from thinking they are worth more money, is to keep them in doubt of the fact that they are performing well in management's eyes.

Oftentimes, when one of these people decides to find a new job and resign, it comes as a tremendous shock to their employer. Reactions like, "Bill, I thought you were happy here! What can I do to keep you?" come way too late! This is an oft-occurring problem that happens so much that employment counselors make an excellent living just serving the unappreciated masses! When someone inquires about an advertised position, it takes but a few minutes to make them realize how unhappy they really are with their present job, and how this is the opportunity that is made for them!

Quite often people who are feeling under-appreciated, or just otherwise restless, will periodically check the newspaper or online for positions of interest. Sometimes just to check and see what jobs similar to theirs are paying. Let a good employment counselor field a call from one of these curiosity seekers, and the selling starts.

I remember just really getting excited when someone would call *just out of curiosity*! When they called in, they maybe were just curious, but by the time we talked awhile, I normally would be able to help them to realize *how unhappy they really were*! If I could ask the right questions, and act surprised that their situation did not include the benefits of the job I was advertising, it wasn't difficult to attract them to come in for an interview. If you make people feel appreciated and compliment them for their talents, they will rush in to meet you, and if for nothing else than to just feel good about being wanted and valuable!

I really haven't analyzed it for years, but I know for a fact that less than thirty percent of all workers could be truthfully said to be happy with their jobs!

When I was an employment counselor, there were no personal computers, cellphones, or any of our current luxuries. Entire industries are now available for job seekers that did not exist back then, but the fact remains that people have not changed much. The basic principles still apply regardless of the jobs offered.

Although I did not necessarily specialize, I had great success with certain groups. One of which was professional truck drivers. There are a lot of long haul truckers out there who get married, begin having children, and after a while, have a great desire to get off the road, and understandably want to be there to see the kids grow up.

So when they see an ad for a warehouse foreman or manager with a requirement for familiarity with big rigs and knowledge of trucking, and a similar income to what they are presently making, the urge is too great not to call; the ideal, *be home every night* job!

The next step was to entice the caller to come in for an interview to see if he matches what the employer is looking for. Now generally, there is more than just the long haul boredom that makes someone start looking elsewhere for another job doing the same thing.

My objective in the interview was to first of all ask enough questions to ascertain all of the reasons the applicant was unhappy and wanted a change. Maybe it was some small reason that had magnified. Maybe he felt passed over when the owner's son got the dispatcher's job that the applicant felt he had earned by his years of service. Here again is a lost opportunity by an employer who could have saved a loyal employee by a quick meeting to let them in on the change they were making, and to express how valuable this person is in their current job, and therefore the reason they did not get the promotion! Maybe a small raise would be enough to retain them.

Whatever the reason, I had to find it and empathize with his unhappiness and feeling of being unappreciated! The next thing I needed to do was go over his application with him in depth. Here I had to really dig into his life. Just like selling a home, or a car, I needed every single *selling feature* he had, as if he was a product I was going to present to a buyer. In reality, he was!

If he belonged to clubs, churches, his hobbies, absolutely everything. Every positive thing about this individual and maybe things his family did not even know! I needed all of his selling features.

Also during this interview, I looked for his *hot buttons*; the thing that he really liked about his current job, as well as the things that he did not care for. It might be something as major as having to *lump* his own loads(unload his own truck upon arrival), or something as minor as his dispatcher having an insulting attitude, or maybe the company having upgraded the rigs some of the newer guys were driving while he still struggled with the same old truck! Typical of so many jobs, such as new office furniture for a junior employee, while the *old timer* makes do with what she has because she has more concern about saving the company money, and as a consequence, is not considered as important to upgrade!

Next, after this exhaustive interview, I seated him in the waiting room and retreated to my office. Now my job really began! Of course, there was no warehouse job, and he wouldn't likely have qualified anyway. So while he thinks I'm calling the employer to schedule his interview, I am calling other companies. Who would I call?

Trucking companies of course! Trucking companies are always in need of good, reliable, and experienced drivers, so I called until I got an interview for him. I used care in my selections, to make sure that I was hopefully placing him with a good company, and one that maybe had something his present company did not. Maybe one that would give him a chance at the dispatcher's job in the future, or less road time out of state, whatever.

Here, I would use the information I gleaned from our interview, and try my best to use his hot buttons as a guide. Maybe the idea of a new truck, or a friendly and caring female dispatcher, or never having to lump another load. Maybe just a feeling of importance when I stress how well respected this new company is and how fortunate he should feel to even have them want to meet him!

Remember that we are dealing with a professional teamster who is good at what he does and mainly just bored with life. My next move is to bring him back to my office, and with great excitement, I take away the warehouse job by describing the employer as misleading us as to hours, pay, or whatever. I'd go on to say, "Naturally, we can't disclose who the company is, but you can be sure we are through representing them, since that job was not what it was supposed to be."

Then I explained that, "I was so upset that the job wasn't what we thought. I sat there disgusted, and then I remembered a great job for a driver that just came in! Now for the good news!" I went on to say, "So I called them on your behalf, and I liked what I heard so much, I set up an interview for you!"

By the way, don't forget that I used every bit of hype that I had from my interview so the employer was looking forward to meeting my applicant, and now I made my applicant look forward to meeting his soon to be new boss!

Now, as far as the fees were concerned, sometimes I could get the employer to pay my fees, or possibly reimburse part of them, or the employee had to pay. We arranged for payroll deduction plans, and many ways for the person to handle the charges.

Consider this; the applicant came in for one job, ended up going to a different job doing the same work they were already doing, only for a different company. Maybe even for the same income, and gladly paid a healthy fee to do it! Why?

This is human nature. People need to change to keep things interesting! They don't necessarily need a new job — they need a new environment!

Before my client left my office, I prepared him extensively on how to get the job. Right down to the proper body language, posture, questions and answers. I supplied the person with every tool and even the script to deliver. It was like being the director of a one act play.

Did I do the job for my client? You bet I did! I made him feel good about his new job, took him away from his drudgery, and his new employer knew more about him from day one than his old employer ever did! Now you know how that dog walks!

What I taught these people, I will share with you! Let this thought stay with you, as perhaps someday when you are getting bored with your job, you may not need a change of occupation, as much as you may just need to do your same job for a new company.

Far too often, people end up trying entire new careers only to find that they hate them; when if they just stayed within their experience level with a change of scenery, they would be extremely happy.

I personally believe in exploring new companies as a way to learn new skills, and adding to your knowledge will make you even more valuable in the future should you have even better opportunities.

GARY and WENDY SWANSON

3 TALK TO THE MIRROR

What is your idea of searching for a job where there are no employment companies involved? Perhaps the state or county employment department? Maybe one of the many online job posting sites or your local newspaper?

These are all good places to begin to look for a job, in addition to your networking with those you already know, but first you need to prepare yourself so that you can compete with others seeking the same position and win!

The job market is tough now and you may have a lot of competition, but it always has been difficult finding a job in many fields!

Now, let's start getting serious about finding a job for you!

Are you going to just run down the street and paper businesses with your resume? Do you plan to fill out volumes of applications in the hope that one may by chance land in front of someone who gives a damn?

First, the *check up from the neck up!* Let's formulate a plan of attack. The mental checkup is what we are concerned with first. You must be mentally prepared!

Do you have a professional resume neatly typed with no creases, fingerprints, or grammatical errors on it? This you must do. There are scads of samples on the internet, so take care of that before anything else.

First of all, list your credentials, and don't forget any achievements, awards, or special recognition that you have achieved, and write down everything that makes you different or special!

Keep in mind that you will only have one chance to make that all-important *first impression!* If you don't do well on your first interview, there won't be another!

Now take some time talking to your mirror. Yes, just the two of you — you and your mirror. Look at the image facing you. Concentrate on you as you sell yourself to you! Would you hire you? If you don't feel comfortable talking to yourself, think about how stupid you'll look in a prospective employer's eyes if you start tripping over your tongue. I'm exaggerating now, as I really want you to practice this one on one! If you like you, the employer will also like you.

This next part is so critical, but it now involves one of the most overlooked and the least understood aspects of job hunting!

Your personal appearance! How do you appear to other people? Even your closest friends cannot be counted on to tell you the truth, so don't even ask them. Why? Because they aren't selling you! You are selling you! Let's go extreme now; for both the men and women.

For the women: No matter what job you are applying for in the business world, you need to dress as professionally as you can. You may say, "This goes without saying," but you wouldn't believe how some women dress for interviews!

Leave the short skirts, excessively high heels, and designer hosiery for the evening. The best thing is to dress well, but plain and as non-provocative as you can!

You may be trying to be sexually attractive to the man who is interviewing you, and batting your eyes, and flirting with him, and thinking you're scoring points, when he suddenly gets a page to the office, and when he returns, he quickly dismisses you with a, "We'll let you know." What happened?

The page he had was his wife, who works in the central office, and when he walked in she calmly told him, "Get rid of her!" You, in the meantime leave, and never know why you didn't get a job you were perfectly qualified for!

I cannot emphasize this strongly enough; don't be too pretty or too flashy! Be clean, be neat, and be professional. I've hired hundreds and hundreds of people in my career, and when a woman comes on too strong on the initial interview, she will, in most every case end up being a liability! I have seen cases where friends have hired sexy looking women for their businesses, and the first trip their wife makes to the business, the new person's future can be put on the calendar.

I think I have covered it enough, but just dress conservatively, be business-like, and you will do well! Just in case I haven't thoroughly addressed this issue, I asked Wendy to write the last section of this chapter from a woman's point of view.

Now for the men: Your preparation may be a lot harder than for the ladies; you are more likely to need more of a thorough detail. You know, like detailing a car before you sell it.

Men have a natural tendency to be less concerned about their appearance, because they are more likely to dress like the friends they hang around with.

So now, when they decide to seek new employment, they may need to make some major adjustments in their wardrobe and appearance. Men also may have a more dramatic variety of differences in employment categories and accepted appearance.

For instance, your crowd may all have shoulder length hair and your present or previous employer allowed it. Now however, you wish to make a career change, and since in your present position, you allowed your hair to lengthen steadily over the last five years, you may be in for a surprise. You were a lot neater in appearance when you first hired on, and now by certain standards, you may be out of style for their business.

Your last employer accepted your change in appearance because you grew on each other. Now, you are starting over so to speak, so be cautious. Look around the area where you live, casually check out the other men who work at your new targeted employer, and see how their hair length is.

Also be aware, just like in your case, their boss may not like their appearance, but he tolerates it; so don't forget; they already *have the job*! You need to earn it! So cut your hair, and once you have a job, grow it out if you still desire! One thing I can assure you of though; unless your head is covered with tattoos, your hair can never be *too* short!

For an example of another kind; let's say that you are an automobile technician (mechanic). You work on engines for a living, and you are applying for a technician's position at another dealership. You maybe haven't had clean fingernails for years. It sure would be a smart idea to clean yourself up when you are applying for a new job!

If I am interviewing a trainer for my horse stable, I do not expect this trainer to apply for the job with horseshit on his boots.

WENDY SAYS, "YOU CAN'T WEAR THAT!"

So ladies, what are you going to wear to that all important interview? Let's go over your grooming from head to toe. Remember, you want to show your potential employer what skills and knowledge you will bring to their company and how you will be a valuable addition. You don't want to be just a pretty face, or a sexy body; you don't want to come off as a distraction.

Do you have long hair? If so, pull it up or away from your face; not a complicated up-do, just a professional looking French twist, a tidy ponytail or bun. Do you have your hair colored professionally or do it yourself? Make sure, you've had your roots touched up just before the interview. No matter what length your hair is, make sure it is styled simply and neatly. Under no circumstances are you to touch your hair during the interview; no patting, smoothing, twisting or fussing with your hair.

Should you wear makeup? Do you normally wear makeup? If the answer is yes, then by all means wear it. Stick to *neutral shades* that are flattering to your skin tone. When it comes to eyeliner, refrain from using it under your eyes; and don't use mascara on your lower lashes. Skip the blush, and you should not wear red lipstick; remember, neutral is the key.

Are your ears pierced more than once per ear? Wear one pair of *small* earrings only. No chandeliers or big hoops; keep to studs, small hoops or drop earrings.

Do you have any facial piercings? Please, please remove that type of jewelry. Even if it's just a small stud in your nose, you don't want the interviewer to spend the time wondering if you really have a piercing or if it's glued on. If you have to ask if you should remove your tongue stud, you are beyond my help!

Do not wear perfume. For one reason, your interviewer may have allergies. Also, what smells great to one person may be unpleasant to someone else. The last thing you want to happen is for your interview to be rushed through because you are in an enclosed space with someone who doesn't care for your scent.

If you are applying for a job in an office, it is best to wear a skirt with a matching blouse and jacket. A dress, again with a jacket is also acceptable, but you should try to avoid wearing slacks. If you must wear slacks, make sure they are the type that has a crease in them.

If you are applying for a job in a more casual setting, for instance a factory, teachers or nurses aid or casual restaurant, a skirt, slacks or dress without a jacket are perfectly fine. The hem of your slacks should come to just the tops of your shoes, about a half an inch above the ground; no capris or ankle pants.

Where ever you are applying, avoid any garment that glitters, sparkles, or shows too much skin. You're not going on a date, but you are trying to get a job. Wear clothing that fits you. Your skirt or dress should at least go to your knees. Your blouse or dress should not show cleavage, be sleeveless, be sheer or too tight. If you wonder if you're showing too much skin, you are. Are your bra straps showing? No, don't forego the bra, but do find a different blouse to wear. Avoid *top shots* when leaning forward.

Make sure your clothing is well pressed. If it is something that is going to look wrinkled after sitting down for a while, like a linen skirt, find something else to wear.

Solid colors will work best; preferably gray, navy or blue. If you wear a black suit, soften it with a pastel or cream colored blouse. Avoid bright colors and patterns, except as a small accent, like a scarf.

A tasteful, unobtrusive necklace is okay. Wear a watch, but avoid bracelets and bangles. If you belong to a professional organization, a small lapel pin is good. Do not wear flashy jewelry, and do not wear anything that symbolizes religion or political affiliation.

Now about your nails; they should be neatly trimmed and not overly long, and above all, clean. Just like your makeup, stick to neutral polish colors and don't add any bling.

Do wear pantyhose; sheer or opaque is fine, but avoid those with patterns. If you need to wear a foundation garment or shapewear, do so.

Finally, we're to your toes. A pump with a small heel is your best choice. Again, a neutral color works best; black, brown or tan. Just like breast cleavage, toe cleavage should also be avoided. So no peep toes, sandals, flats, boots, platforms, and above all, no sneakers, in fact, nothing with laces. Your shoes should be clean and well maintained. Use a leather or suede cleaner to get them looking their best. Use some shoe polish if necessary. Don't forget to look at the bottoms of your shoes; did you forget to remove the price tag or any other markings?

Do you have tattoos? If so, hopefully they are below the neck. If they're on your arms or chest, make sure they're covered by your clothing. If they're on the lower portion of your legs, wear opaque hose.

So now you think you're ready for that interview. Check yourself out in the mirror, head to toe and front to back. Is your slip showing? Are you ready for an interview with the president of the United States or your state governor? Smile; do you have lipstick on your teeth? Walk around the room and back to the mirror. Are you still put together? Now, place a chair in front of the mirror and sit down. Do you still look professional? Are there any gaps in your blouse, or is your skirt too tight, or are you showing too much of anything? Are you sitting up straight on the edge of your chair with your legs together? You should be. Don't get too comfortable, and never, never cross your legs!

Overall, your aim is to appear confident, reliable, and competent. By dressing conservatively you will display that you are serious about your profession and getting a job.

4 BE A QUITTER

This chapter is for smokers only; non-smokers are enviously excused from the sufferers, unless you have a friend or loved one who smokes. You may find a way to help them. Otherwise for the non-smokers, see you in the next chapter.

This is the only time in this book that it is good to be a quitter!

If you are a smoker, *do not* have any cigarettes before your interview! That doesn't mean one last one just before entering the business! This means don't smoke one after you are dressed for your interview. Do not smoke until your interview is over and you have left the premises!

As a former chain smoker, I can smell a cigarette smoker from twenty feet away! Even smokers can smell other smokers, and it will kill you on an interview for many sales positions, and a lot of other businesses where you spend time inside a building with others.

Non-smokers today have a very intolerant attitude toward smokers. Much more than it used to be when half of us smoked! I know how hard it is to quit, so those who don't smoke may skip the next chapter, as this information is only understandable for those who have the habit.

This is the only bad habit that I gave up that was truly enjoyable. That's why it is so great to no longer be enslaved by it!

This is tough to do! I know, because I quit 533 times before I finally figured out the system! This is nothing complicated; in fact, it's so easy it's crazy that I took so long to figure it out. Now don't get me wrong, when I say easy, that's because I suffered so much trying everything else first.

Your first step to quitting is to make certain you have a few packs of cigarettes on hand. Why? Think about it — How panicky are you going to be if you are sitting there at 10:00 at night, and you are feelin' tweaky? You start to shake just thinking about it! The nearest convenience store closes at 11:00 P.M. and it's just a short walk of a couple of blocks.

So, just in case, you may stroll over and you feel by the time you get there you may have talked yourself out of it, at least in the worst case scenario, you will just buy a pack to have on hand and won't even consider opening it. WRONG! I did it hundreds of times; same exact plan; the minute I walked out of the store, I was tearing open the pack and walking happily home with a pleased look on my face! No more panic, no more depression; life was good! That's why you need smokes on hand!

One pack for the car, one pack in your desk in the office, some at home, and don't forget lighters! Cigarettes without lighters cause even more panic! I hope I am talking now to the confirmed smokers, because the occasional, part-timers will not understand!

Over the years I have done it all — I even gave up coffee for six months once, while I was quitting, and was able to put cigarettes behind me for seventeen and a half years! Then one night, after a tough and long day, I was having a cocktail with a friend who was smoking, and it just hit me hard! I wanted to really relax, and drink, and smoke. But only a couple. Then I told myself, "I'll never smoke again."

In those days, bartenders sold cigarettes and we smoked indoors. This happened at 9:00 P.M. When I went to bed that night, I had two cigarettes left for my morning. On my way to work, I stopped at the store, purchased two cartons of Winstons, two Bic lighters, a Zippo (a fancy one) and fuel; and that day I smoked three and a half packs. From that time on, I settled down to a regular two and a half to three packs per day for the next 15 years!

You know, the strange thing about this re-start program was I had expected to get light-headed, or cough, or something, but no; it was just like I had never quit, and that was after 17 ½ years! I have been off the chokes about eight years now, but I am a cigarette addict! I know if I smoked one, that I would be headed to the store for cartons and lighters! There is no permanent cure. Once you get it done, just never, ever try one again!

This was the most enjoyable habit I ever had! The negatives were; when I got colds, they lasted and turned into pneumonia four times! I stunk, my home stunk, my car stunk, my hair stunk, and I look back on myself as well-dressed and professional looking, but smelling like a repulsive slob! In today's society, smoking is a ten times bigger detriment than it was when I did it! Besides, I used the excuse that I was in a high pressure environment! That was a good excuse that lasted me until I finally discovered a way out!

The prescription for quitting — Purchase a box of nicotine patches, in fact, you will need more than that! I bought three. Begin by making sure you are well supplied with cigarettes also, and never allow yourself to not have your smokes and lighter nearby!

Begin by starting your first day with the heaviest dose patch as the company recommends. Next, place a second heavy-dose patch in your wallet or your purse, and one in your glove box. You also need to have another at your place of employment, along with your backup cigarettes! You may be starting to question my sanity, but remember; I am addressing the hardcore, dedicated, and addicted smoker who has tried to quit and failed!

This is the hardest thing you likely will ever attempt, so damned well listen to me! There will come a time when you are in a hurry, and jump out of the shower, and be halfway to work when you discover you forgot your patch! With your backup smokes being always close at hand, you will be oh so glad that you have a backup nicotine patch! Get it on right away. Don't wait 'til you get to work; do it now! The first thing you do when you get home that night will be to replace your backup patch, wherever you pulled it from!

I stayed on the heaviest dosage twice as long as the company recommended, and then when I finally got to the low level, I stayed on them three times longer than they suggested! I still carried backup nicotine patches for several years after I quit smoking, and I know never to tempt fate again!

Oh, the new e-cigarettes? Forget it! You can go suck automobile exhaust pipes too, but it won't work.

Back in the days, everyone made a big deal out of substitutes for smoking. The experts all claimed it was a learned response that could be cured by substituting for the pacifier effect! What a crock! I ate hundreds upon hundreds of plastic pens, toothpicks, and every other asinine substitute, but it all came down to a plain and simple nicotine addiction!

Do it my way, and it will likely save or prolong your life and allow you to have better relationships and a better life! Besides, it will most certainly allow you to enjoy a better career path in most all cases!

Wow! After all of this sales pitch, I almost feel a need for a patch! Fortunately, I no longer even need to carry them. Join me!

GARY and WENDY SWANSON

5 WHY PEOPLE CHANGE JOBS

We have already looked at some of the reasons why people change jobs, and when we look at the type of work they feel they would enjoy, it seems that it is not all too different from what they are doing at the present time.

Take the early example of the long haul trucker who responded to the warehouse foreman position. I might mention that this was not an isolated instance; this was an ad I regularly ran, and the same scenario repeated on a weekly basis! Men came in to interview for a warehouse foreman position, and ended up happily working for a new trucking company!

Then there is the case of the hair salon manager, the office manager, executive secretary, and the list just continues off the page! When you analyze human nature, you soon see that the majority of people in the work force that have had a few years out of school seem to gravitate toward that which is familiar to them, but also at what they consider to be the next level in their progression toward happiness.

Using the example of the employment company, the reason these methods were so successful is the feel-good factor!

After being with most companies for a while, learning their job, and then repeating the same procedures day after day, and month after month, the years seem to roll by, and sooner or later people start to analyze their lives.

Sometimes, just a simple and sudden back pain at the end of a long day can trigger a self-analysis. That's when we say to ourselves, "Oh, I'm getting to old for this s…!" If we haven't said it ourselves, we've all heard someone say that, and doesn't it make you think of your future with your company if someone who has been there longer than you is making this comment? You bet it does!

If your fellow employee is feeling this way, and you are doing the same job, this is naturally a red flag; isn't it? If Bob feels like that now, and he probably only stays because he feels he's too old to find a new job, are you thinking, "Will I feel this same way when I get to be his age?" This causes a lot of consternation and soul-searching in people, and much of it is unnecessary!

Maybe Bob had a previous career that he had gone to school for, and was doing very well climbing the ladder until he finally reached what I call *progressive incompetence*. Bob maybe got one too many promotions than he should have, and the last promotion was just "over his head," and neither he nor his employer had any way out but to part company. Had they been able to reverse everything, they would have both been happy, but now it's too late. Bob had failed in both of their eyes and left.

So don't let Bob's failure affect your career. Pride has a lot to do with this type of failure! I have known hundreds of people all across the United States whose competency I have wondered about. It is a normal part of corporate structures that most every individual is continually seeking the next level! The old saying to junior executives is, "With your credentials and our great company, you have nowhere to go but up!" Just don't try to go further than your ability!

You can just see the newly hired executive moving into one of the thirty desks on an office floor, amid twenty-nine other people who all dress alike, look alike, and act alike. He goes home all excited that first night and says, "Honey, my boss told me that I am certain to go up the ladder!" From that time on, the employee works very hard for the next promotion and then the next one, and from the beginning, where he had to compete with twenty-nine others, and then only fifteen at the next juncture, and ne moves up again to where he is now one of only five vice-presidents at the upper level of management! This type of corporate progression is normal.

Since he has done so well, he now deserves an identity; so let's call him Don! Don is finding that each promotion has been successively more difficult. That's normal, what good is a promotion without greater and more difficult responsibility? But maybe, just maybe, this current level should be Don's last.

Let's say that he has had a real tough time grasping the new concepts and duties. He has been called in by his superior on numerous occasions and it has taken a long time, and many mistakes for him to be able to feel competent in this position. Naturally, his peers know nothing of his previous difficulties, and perhaps his errors and problems have been brushed over and covered up by his immediate supervisor. Let's say at this level that Don's boss is the executive vice-president, and he did not confess to the company president that he had made a bad decision in recommending that Don be promoted. Let's further assume that the exec has had problems making proper decisions in the past, and he has managed to cover up and bury all of Don's mistakes. Everyone in the company thinks Don is a great vice-president and this includes Don himself!

Executives oftentimes feed off of their own importance. Don maybe thought all of those *beat up* sessions with his boss were a normal occurrence for vice-presidents and maybe he really thought that everything was fine! The exec's covering up for Don hurt them both.

Now, the big day comes for Don! The company suddenly announces that the executive vice-president will no longer be coming in, as he is *pursuing other interests*! This means that he was fired!

Now, as I said, Don's boss, the executive vice president, had been having problems for a long time. He had been making mistakes all along, and was finally dismissed by the company. One of the greater mistakes had been in promoting Don to vice president! He had continually covered for Don, and the president and the board were totally unaware of the long series of mistakes and cover-ups that the exec made in order to keep Don's inability to handle his job from becoming evident. This would have been the last straw for both of them.

Now you see the picture; as to how by covering up a bad hiring decision, affected the entire operation. However, the cover-up entailed many discussions of "What a good job Don was doing!"

Certainly unexpected, and a shock to everyone from Don's level down, the dismissal so near the top is a real and total surprise!

This is common in the corporate world. Companies normally do not breathe a word to a person's underlings prior to their dismissal! If they have not quietly, and of course confidentially, enlisted the services of a head hunter, there is now a job opening for executive vice-president!

Remember, the former exec was dismissed! You know he's not going to do anything to stop the semi-incompetent Don from getting promoted to his job! Just the opposite; if the company is making a generous separation offer (to avoid bad press and lawsuits, because corporations don't have a heart), it is very likely that the outgoing executive will highly recommend our man Don to take over the number two spot in the company! Since the president and the board have been sheltered from any knowledge of Don's past failures, it is highly probable that the terminated exec has planted a costly time bomb in his former company! "Here's to you as a parting gift boss," he thinks, as he walks out the door!

At this point Don let's his ego control his acts, and when the four vice-presidents are interviewed by the president and the board of directors, he unashamedly admits to having *helped his former boss by doing a lot of his work.* Who's to know, since the last exec won't even talk to them? Don now does a beautiful job of accomplishing his final dream, albeit a short one!

This scenario happens so often and destroys so many people that could otherwise have enjoyed a lasting and rewarding career! As Clint Eastwood said to his soon to be ex-boss, "A man's got to know his limitations!"

Next time you hear someone utter the, "I'm too old for this s…," just remember, they may have come down hard on the elevator of failure, and it's often a lot faster than climbing the stairs to the top.

Don't be a SNIOP (susceptible to the negative influence of other people). You have your own self to take care of, and what some people hate in this life, others love!

Find something that you enjoy, and pursue it! Do what you want to do! I know many happy people who, after climbing the corporate ladder at one company, rose higher than their ability, and after a period of mourning for their lost egos was over, started at a similar company and rose to where their competence level was at its' zenith, and they stayed happily at that level from then on.

Sometimes peer pressure and false egos push people to move up the ladder until they reach that level where they cease to excel, and instead, may barely be able to hang on to their position. Plus that, they cannot step back to their old job without losing face; and instead they flounder until they are forced to leave the company entirely.

By now, you may have noticed a trend and an underlying message. There is a big lesson to be learned by observation of others.

You should now realize after all of this, that the greater part of our entire work force is not all that happy with their work! However, the elementary reason that people are unhappy may not be the fault of the job itself, but of the people who they work for! Will Rogers said, "Thank God you and I are different; otherwise one of us would be unnecessary!"

I have found a lot of people over the years that I would lump in that unnecessary category. You know the type I mean — always criticizing everyone and everything! At first observation, one would figure them to be a waste of skin, but when you get to know them better, you may just find out that this is just their way of being noticed. Maybe they tried being nice, but felt that people were taking advantage of them, so this way they get negative attention instead of none at all. Everyone wants to be noticed.

Back to your needs, now that we know what you face when you apply for a job! Use this knowledge to your advantage. Remember that you have two ears and only one mouth, so it makes sense that you should listen twice as much as you talk!

The trick is to get your interviewer to open up and do more talking than they usually do, and maybe more than they should!

The how to of this move is a major key to getting yourself hired! Think about this person who sits across from you and may ultimately decide your destiny! Here is an employee who is likely to be unappreciated to a certain degree. The job of the initial interviewer is not all that important, unless you are applying to a smaller company and the person across from you is also the decision maker.

So, if this person does not make the final decision, your goal is to get to the next step, isn't it? You must somehow impress this first line of defense enough to get to the ultimate decider. How? Easier than you could ever imagine; but you must be a good actor for this next part: Now we schmooze!

Be very careful at this point, because you cannot fake sincerity. Yes, that's right. Just convince yourself that the person across from you is the *big boss*! He or she may as well be, because they will really decide if you progress to the next step, or place your tail between your legs and go home!

Now, you need to be as sincere as you were to that traffic cop you tried to convince that you weren't really texting, you were just shutting off your cellphone! There will be times in your interview when you will have an opportunity to schmooze, and suck up like crazy! A compliment that will make your interviewer feel good will work wonders if it is sincere, but you'd better be able to pull it off, or you're toast! You can't sound like you're pandering; even though you are!

Be ever so careful, but find something about the person you can truly like and honestly be appreciative of! Forget all about phony compliments on their dress, hairstyle, or

GARY and WENDY SWANSON

anything personal. "I love your cologne," doesn't even go over in a bar, so don't try it on someone in an interview!

You can pay a compliment to someone indirectly by applauding their employer. Saying, "I've heard that it's very hard to get a job with your company because they have a reputation of being so good to work for!" "You compliment my company, you compliment me!"

Never forget that you may very well be sitting across from one of those unappreciated and pigeon-holed folks that haven't been shown any real appreciation for years for what they do. They don't actually feel good about themselves because they are taken for granted! Now you come along with a genuine respect for their position, and you just became a cause for a *feel good* moment. Just some small and sincere showing of respect for their position can almost assure you of that second interview!

I have sat in many interviews over the years where I was brought in to replace a person, but the company had a policy where no one was hired for management from *the outside*. All promotions came from within.

So here I am sitting in front of the person whom I will soon replace, and I have to act innocent and pretend I have no management experience! In actuality, I am far better qualified than the person telling me how great he is, and I have to play dumb while I play along with his huge ego trip, while internally, I am thinking that when I take over, I may not even allow him to remain with the company and work for me!

I'm sure you can find something to like about your interviewer. Again, look around and be observant. People adorn their offices with the things of which they are the most proud. It's never rude to find a time during your interview to walk over to take a closer look at a diploma, an award, team photo, family vacation photo, graduation photo, or who knows what may be displayed. Pay attention; you are seeing the important things in this person's life! Just make sure this is your interviewer's office and not just one he or she borrowed.

If they didn't want people to notice, they wouldn't display them; so by noticing and asking questions, you are paying them a compliment. Male grouse don't display their plumage and beat their wings to not attract attention! People don't wear a heavy Rolex to just tell time! Egos like to be fed! Don't be phony and over nourish someone's ego, but feel free to make sure it gets plenty to eat!

GARY and WENDY SWANSON

6 RESEARCH THE OTHER GUY'S NEEDS

Research before you leap! All too often, we discover things during or after an interview that if we had known them up front, it may have made a difference in our discussion.

We need to spend some time learning about a company that we wish to work for. Why even go through that door if you don't want to work there? Do you go in without a clue as to what they are all about? Unfortunately, many people do!

As an employer, I want someone to show me they really want to work for me. I don't want some poor slob who says, "Yeah man, I just wanted to see if you've got any jobs. I'll do most anything, 'cause I really need money!"

Now, what do you think an employer's reaction will be to that sort of pitch? If you want to work for a company that will hire most anyone who has a pulse or can fog a mirror, what kind of future will it hold? I realize that when one needs a job, we will do most anything in order to have money coming in so we can continue to search for a better job. Without any amount of research, you may as well drop hire-me leaflets from high-rise buildings for all the good you will do!

In today's world, there is so much information available on most every company, that a few minutes at a computer will yield a potential secret to finding that job! Even if you don't own a computer, the local library will have one available.

Let's say that you hear that the Excelsior Company is hiring at their Parkway office. Knowing where it is, and being dressed quite well at the time, you decide to stop in and check it out. You walk into an impressive office and speak to the secretary who asks to help, and you ask her if they have any job openings. She says, "This is your lucky day! Mr. Wells is the one who does the hiring, and he just got back from a trip, so no one has been interviewed yet!" You're then ushered into a comfortable office and Mr. Wells greets you with a warm handshake, and you take the proffered seat.

Mr. Wells says, "I understand that you came about the job, may I see your resume?" Now, since you had not been prepared, and had not checked ahead to even call the company to confirm that there even was an opening; you are at a decided disadvantage aren't you? You don't even know what job is available, nor are you even prepared to be interviewed. In Mr. Well's eye, you are just some Joe off the street who is looking for *any* job!

Now, you may be able to recover with some fast reaction, like, "I'm sorry sir; I didn't take time to bring my resume; as I was leaving work someone said your company had an opening, and since your company has such a great reputation, I just rushed to get here as soon as I could!" Now that may just do the trick if you can react that fast! Most people can't; they absolutely fumble that football and their game is over!

Be prepared! More jobs are lost by people who would be perfect candidates, but they fail to properly sell themselves. When you are looking for work, you are a door to door salesperson. That's right! You have one product to sell; you! Just like any salesperson, you had better know how your product will benefit the person and the company to whom you are trying to sell it!

If you come to me for a job, you'd better impress the livin' hell out of me, because in today's market I have lots to choose from; don't I? If I ask you why you want this job, don't give me the old garbage about needing a job to feed your family! Consider me as someone who cares only about his company. When I interview you, I don't care about your needs; I care about mine, right? You don't get jobs based on sympathy! You get jobs based on what you bring to the table! I may be the most benevolent person on the planet, but when you apply to me for a job, we had both better be concerned with what I want, and only my wants!

The employer will choose the applicant who can do the most for them. They give little sway to the person who has a family to support, and very often will choose a single person for many positions because in larger firms, a person without family responsibilities is a lot easier to call on for longer hours, sudden trips out of town, and even promotions! A single person can most often transfer at the drop of a hat, and the company will not have the additional expenses and delays that moving an entire family involve.

I have been transferred with promotions that the company really invested a lot of money to accomplish! Moving companies to pack the entire home, and to unpack at the new home and put everything away in drawers and closets! Every toothpick, fork, spoon, and knife individually wrapped, shipped, unwrapped, and put away in the new home. There was even a billiard table to disassemble, ship and a professional billiard company to reassemble it at the new place. You can safely add over two thousand dollars for this part alone! Months in motels with meals, laundry, and all necessities completely paid; all waiting for the new home to be readied! Even the real estate commissions being paid! The extra costs for employers who transfer families can easily reach thirty to sixty thousand dollars, and much more; not to even mention the salary increases necessary to entice the employee to make the move!

So, now maybe you can see why using the *family to support* line may not always be a good idea, especially with larger firms where you are applying for an executive position.

The answer in seeking employment that makes the most sense of anything, is to adopt the attitude of, "Mr. Employer, here's what I can do for you!" That is really the bottom line in all of your job searching isn't it? What do you have to offer someone?

In our last example, if you rush headlong into an interview without advance preparation, you had better be fast on your feet, or you will lose!

Now, let's get back to your research. Before you go on an interview, do your research. Learn all you can about the company you are going to apply to.

What is their purpose? Who owns it, and where do the owner's reside?

Find out if this is a locally owned company, or if not, where is its' home office, and why do they own this location.

Is it due to an acquisition, or how does this operation tie in with the mother company? Do they fill a different need, or are they a previous competitor that was purchased to control the market?

Maybe you wish to go further, depending on the position you will be seeking? How does their Dunn and Bradstreet rating look?

Better Business Bureaus won't tell much about employers, because they are all members of the BBB and you seldom ever see anything negative written on that forum! They never seem to comment negatively on their business members. It would be like Al Capone being criticized by his nightclub manager — It just ain't gonna' happen!

Get as much background as you can on any company that you may wish to work for. Look for the good! Find something that you can like about this company and be sure to incorporate it into your interview.

GARY and WENDY SWANSON

7 NOW YOUR RESEARCH GETS PERSONAL

Oh, there's more research? You bet there is; so let's look at you from the employer's standpoint.

When you look out on today's job market, you have to ask yourself what you hope to accomplish when you walk through the door to a company for the first time.

Do you just want to take your interviewer's time to tell you all about their company and why they would really appreciate you coming to work for them?

Is your intent to walk through the door and shout, "Your prayers are answered, I'm here!" You say, "No." Okay then, what is your reason for being unprepared? Your answer, "None!" Good answer! Now we understand each other.

You and I need to be on the same song sheet! This brings us to your research that must be done before any interview takes place; if you intend to get hired!

If you apply to me for a job, don't expect me to try to sell you on why you should work for me! Remember me? I'm the one hiring, so I hope you will be able to impress the hell out of me by giving me some good reasons as to why you really want to work for me!

Don't expect me to even blink if your reason is, to feed your family or you really need a job! I want to hear how you have heard what a great company I have! I will respond to, "All of my friends say they and their families all recommend your firm!" Your needs are not important to me! My needs are the reason I am interviewing you! It is my needs that you had better be concerned with! We'll talk about your needs after you have impressed me by first of all telling me why you selected my company to apply to *first*. I do wish to hear about your future plans as you move up in my company and the fact that you hope someday to earn a promotion to my management team! Your job may be to feed my ego until I'm full, and then we can discuss you!

Most employers don't expect you to know all about their company if they have placed a help-wanted ad. They will be impressed however, if you have enough knowledge about their operation to ask specific questions that indicate your recognition of who they are and what they do.

I would suggest that you make some inquiries about their company prior to your interview. Internet searches, businesses in the neighborhood, and even the little mom and pop mini mart around the corner have a good insight into companies in their area, as a lot of the employees are likely to be their customers. A casual question dropped when they're not busy will often give you more information than you ever dreamed about the company you're interested in.

You need a very believable answer as to why you really want to work for this company you are applying at! Something that hits the hot button of the interviewer! Now, all of this may seem strange to someone who has been trying hard to find work, but a high volume of handing out resumes is like campaigning for office. If all you wanted was votes, I can see it, however for employment it seems like a rather sloppy way to go about it!

If you give the impression that you're open to just taking any job, you telegraph a message to the employer that you won't last long. As soon as you find something you like better, you're gone and they're looking for someone else! Not good!

Further preparation of your person is never a waste of time. Depending on the level of employment you are going after, your preparation will change.

When you are scheduled for an interview, make certain that you are properly dressed for the occasion. If you are in doubt, it's *not* the best idea to ask your friends. Friends are always complimentary to their friends, and that's not what you're looking for! You want constructive criticism, not compliments!

When preparing a proper wardrobe for an interview, for a *white* collar position, stop in to a high-end clothing store like Nordstrom and ask for advice. The sales clerk will be complimented by your asking, even if you don't make a purchase. The mere fact that you consider them as the authority will boost their ego and help you. Then, when you start making the big bucks, keep them in mind for your next wardrobe upgrade. Now this applies to white collar work specifically, but proper and clean clothing is a must for any type of work!

It's hard to believe how some people show up for an interview! Nose hair, ear hair, long hair around the eyes and eyebrows looking like gnarly caterpillars on men just makes one wonder if they even have a mirror! You may be applying to dig ditches, but don't show up dirty. Also have on clean footwear. Well-shined shoes are an absolute must for an office position, and for most all interviews. It may be the only time you dress well, but please do so when interviewing.

Your appearance is the first impression you make when meeting someone, so why would you take a chance? Now, let me get insulting for a minute, as there are some people who really need it!

If you are just coming off a several day drunken binge, and your eyes look like pee-holes in the snow, and the booze is still seeping from your pores, stay home!

Many people smell, and a lot of people just plain stink! Think back on the last person you passed in a mall, a store, a bus, the subway, or just anywhere, that you noticed their body odor or cigarette smell enough to make you look to see where it was coming from. No one likes offensive odors and most of us detest foul smells of any kind. If you could gag a maggot, do you really think you can get hired?

When someone who is sitting in judgment of whether or not they change your life by giving you a job, don't be so horribly stupid as to show up smelling like a pile of dog poop! Like I said about smokers — Do not think that you can put out your cigarette, walk in my door and have the audacity to ask me for a job! You stink! Did you know that I am a former smoker and I miss it terribly? Did you know that I am using the nicotine patch and I hate you for reminding me how miserable I am? Do you know that if you wish to conclude this interview outside with both of us smoking, that I'd be all for it! I exaggerate? Don't kid yourself! That would be like going to an AA meeting with an open beer. You want to be lynched?

If you can't relate to this, then congratulations, you are a non-smoker! However, if you are not, you'd better not smoke one within a few hours of meeting me, because sometimes I think I can smell a cigarette a mile away. In fact, I know I can!

The reason I have spent so much time on this subject is because I have cut short many interviews over the years where people have made immediate negative impressions on me. I felt that if this was the best they could do to apply for the job; it would only get worse after I hired them.

I'll repeat this for the hard of seeing; your presence in my office today is, I expect, the best which I likely will ever see you, so therefore, over the term of your employment, this will be as good as it gets! You owe it to yourself to make a good impression.

GARY and WENDY SWANSON

8 YOUR CREDENTIALS ARE SHOWING

When you apply for employment, don't take any chances on not making a good first impression!

What is the value of the resume? This is your *bona fides* so to speak. Your credentials, your whole selling pitch, right? So what do you feel like when you hand it to the interviewer and they open it, scan a few pages, frown slightly, and casually just flip it down on the desk? My question is, "Did the interviewer ask for your resume?" Did you not fill out their application as requested? I ask this because you are the applicant! *You do not* determine in what order the interview is conducted, nor do you control it!

Why the strong emphasis? Because, if this scenario happens to you, your first reaction will be that you are offended by the interviewer's rudeness, and it will show! The interviewer may be offended by your audacity, and tossing your resume aside is his or her way of regaining the control they felt you were exerting! All of this from just handing them your resume? Yes! Do only what you are asked, and don't get too anxious to rush the process.

Besides, do you really want this person to sit and read about you rather than make eye contact while conversing? Of course not! If that were the case, you could have mailed it. In addition to that, what a terrific way to conclude an interview, by handing it to them at the end. Do not ever detract from your opportunity to have a conversation where you can visibly sell yourself and your sincerity, eyeball to eyeball!

Be aware of your posture as well! Both feet on the floor, sitting upright, on the front half of the chair. Save the leaning back, legs crossed posture for after you have earned the right. Your objective here is to have respect for the authority of the one conducting the interview. Even if you know this person is an insignificant person in the company pecking order, they work here and you do not! Most often, you may be the first applicant to show them the courtesies, and they'll love you for it!

Answer questions carefully, and be certain not to overly embellish your accomplishments, because depending on the skill level of the interviewer, the fact that you can type 120 words a minute or are expert with Excel spreadsheets may not register. Maybe they are looking at you for an entirely different position and they are testing you to see how you handle yourself. Don't try to analyze how they want you to answer to fit their needs, just directly respond to the question and be brief.

Trying to second guess the interviewer is a mistake. I have sat there before on interviews where the questioning has suddenly taken a direct opposite tack, and while wondering how in the world we went off on such a tangent, but just kept responding. At the end of a few minutes, the person said, "I think you're over qualified for this position, I'd like to offer you this —." Wow! More money than I dreamed and I walked out a happy camper! This happens a lot, so just *feel the force* and let it flow. Besides, your interviewer may be inexperienced and lost in the process. Be tolerant and courteous.

For this reason, don't worry about a script! Just respond to questions as honestly as you can. Many interviews are well scripted to draw out your inner self, break down your inhibitions, and allow the interviewer to draw out the *real you*. It's truly amazing how often the conversation is all just purposefully designed to get at that secret and unrehearsed *you*!

Psychological tests that I have taken over the years were really in-depth and quite repetitive, because there may be ten like-sounding questions, each with a slightly different twist, all designed to determine your I.Q. and see what level of management you are best at.

I always did them well, and had some record high scores, which I was so proud of that I listed these accomplishments on my resumes for years until I finally got smart and stopped! I found that flaunting my test abilities to show that I qualified to be the interviewer's boss was likely not a good flag to wave! Also, being able to test well doesn't mean you can perform, so it just amounts to a bluff anyway.

Some employers will ask their applicants to take written tests not to make sure they're qualified, but to make sure they can follow directions. This is especially true of technical positions; such as engineers, accountants, data analysts, etc.

Wendy told me about a test that had to be taken before you could even get an interview at a computer software firm. If you didn't answer every question in a set amount of time and score 100% — no interview! She went on to say that the questions weren't difficult, but if you didn't read the instructions at the beginning that told you to mark certain questions as N/A, and others with a specific *wrong* answer, there was no way you could get 100%.

Remember the "I'm here to work for you" concept. No matter what our skill level, we need to humble ourselves enough to show utmost respect for the person conducting the interview, because otherwise we may never get a chance to be their boss!

No need to be phony just be a little humble at this point, because you'll find that many interviewers seem to be jerks! Just like everything else in life, sometimes you just have to shake your head and wonder. Kind of like the boss's son; Daddy says, "Go out there son and fake it 'til you make it!"

You may be asked to give the person a verbal rundown on your past, including your accomplishments, your greatest success, or your worst experience. This is your time to shine! You may want to ask how long you have. It's tough to feel like you just got started when the interviewer holds up her hand and you didn't even get to your best times; so be clear on the time first. If they want the Readers Digest version and you're launching into "War and Peace," it won't fit the timeframe allowed. Basically, what you are asking is, "How long do I have to sell myself?"

Also, when asked to expound on your background, don't you dare bring out that resume! That, you still save! It is your exit visa.

When asked about your previous or present employer, always compliment them, no matter how you truly feel! Never divulge company skeletons, and never bad mouth people or the operation of their business! Let your interviewer knowingly nod when you say, "I'm just looking for a chance to advance my career."

There may come a time when you are confronted with a difficult question as I have been. For example; I went in to this company cold! No opening and they didn't know I was coming. I asked for the owner, and when we shook hands, I told him I wanted a manager's position with his company. His answer was, "We don't have any openings, but if you leave me your resume (he could see it in my hand), I'll call you if we have an opening some time. My next move was crude and gutsy, but I really wanted to work there, as it was the best company in the area. I said, "How many managers do you have in this department now?" He answered, "Four." I said, "Well, I know I can outdo what you have, so give me the weakest manager's job!" After his shock, he invited me into his office. Then after looking at my resume, he looked surprised and said, "You sure have had a lot of jobs!" Knowing I had just one chance at this job, I reacted quickly, and I calmly said, "I was thinking about just circling the companies in the yellow pages, but thought I'd prepare a resume instead!" Of course, this was said with a big smile, and I just stared back at him. He then asked in all sincerity, "How do I know how long you'll stay with me with your track record?" I said, "You don't," and in a low, confident tone, "because I'll stay until I get bored, and during that time I'm with you, I'll make you more money than anyone ever has!" We shook hands, and I started two days later with the other manager working for me! It turned out to be several years of each of us being glad we got together.

I say this not to brag, but to open your eyes and clear up the old job hopper mindset that a lot of employers and job counselors have! As long as you have a plausible explanation for your employment record, you don't have to be afraid to quit! Now this won't apply to every position, as it does depend a lot on the type of work you are in, and when I pulled my brash move, I was applying for a sales manager's position.

If you find out that you made a mistake by hiring on at a place that turns out to be a total disappointment, does some job guru expect you to stay and suffer? Is there some evil sort of job genie out there that insists on you paying for your mistake by suffering for your misjudgment? Forget that!

Besides, here's another way to look at it; if you go to work for a company, learn all you can about it, rise as far as you can without buying the place, is there anything wrong with making a move to another firm where you have room to advance? Show me the person in the dunce cap who dreamed up that philosophy! The only type of people who can find fault with my analysis are those who fit into a mold that I can describe best by a quote from Theodore Roosevelt: *"Far better it is to dare mighty things, to win glorious triumphs, even though checkered with failure, than to take rank with those poor spirits who neither enjoy much, nor suffer much, for they live in that gray twilight that knows neither victory nor defeat!"* This is what I live by and Teddy's enthusiasm has carried me across the United States through jobs I never even thought attainable!

If you show me your track record has a pattern of learning and successful steps, even though you've changed jobs often, as your employer, I will know not to let your life become stagnant! This type of person needs to be constantly challenged and given more responsibility! I like to feed this type with enough challenges that we finally get to the level just before they reach that point where we know they should be cautious about the next step, where they reach their level of progressive incompetence. People and employers can generally tell when they are about at their level of maximum competence.

Naturally there are people out there who change jobs a lot because nobody likes them, but they aren't reading this book. They already know it all!

The last thing you need to do before leaving the interview is to *ask for the job!* This is the absolute best and *most important thing you can do!* Depending on circumstances, you will be asked at the end of the discussion if you have any more questions. Your answer will hinge on the level of comfort that you have reached with your interviewer, and whether or not you are sitting with an underling or the actual decision maker.

I would advise that some of the best answers are, "How soon may I start?" or "Where is the employee parking, I'll get my car moved?" or "What day can I start, and is there any studying I can do beforehand?" Just anything to *trial close,* and always with a smile of course! I will *never* hire someone who won't ask me for the job! ABSOLUTELY NEVER!

If your interviewer says the usual, "Oh, we'll call you," or the like, then be prepared to ask your questions about if there is any studying you can do for the position, and try to enter into some more intelligent dialogue where you ask the type of questions the employer likes to hear. You already should know by this point in the interview whether you want the job. They already discussed the duties and the pay. Don't be too benefit conscious or ask questions about vacations, overtime hours, or other of the type that I would refer to as *job killers.* I feel that way because as an employer, you can impress me enormously by questions like, "Is there self-study material that I can do at home, or can I come in early or stay late so I can get up to speed quickly?" Questions about insurance or benefits are mostly unnecessary at this stage, and can bring up negative thoughts about the cost of hiring you to the employer.

It's not that these benefit type questions should remain unanswered; it's just that they haven't hired you yet, and hopefully, most companies will have comparable benefit packages, so it's not necessary to make a point on this interview of asking too many questions about *how much you can do for me*. Besides, after you are hired, you may discuss all of these questions before you sign your paperwork. Then if it stinks, don't take the job. At that point, you are in the *driver's seat*.

If the interview ends without a decision, that is the time to hand the person your resume with a statement, "May I leave my resume with you? It will give you more information and I can be reached at this number, etc." Hopefully, in the initial greeting you handed the person a *calling card*. This is always impressive, as it denotes class and professionalism!

Many years ago, I was introduced to a friend of a famous speaker, author and lecturer, and as we shook hands, he handed me his card. The card was imprinted with only his name, and it called back memories of a more elegant time. No phone number, nothing but his name; as I said, a calling card.

It might behoove you to have some cards printed, or if you can, do it yourself on your own printer; a small expenditure is a nice touch. Just your name and phone number is all it should have on it; or, just your name. You can always add a number by writing it on the card, and then the person feels even more special! While you're at it, if you have some cutesy voice message on your phone, change it. You don't want your prospective employer calling when you can't pick up and having some foul or stupid voice mail message that totally destroys the impression you left at the company. I've seen it happen. You may as well have a message that says, "Sorry, I changed my mind; I don't really want your job!" It's surprising, the voice mail messages that people keep on their phones that totally defy common sense. Think hard about this, as we personalize our cellphone greetings maybe too much. Also, when interviewing, leave your cellphone in your car!

If another company person comes in to join the interview, you may consider this to be a good sign. Very often, if someone is doing well and making a good impression, the interviewer will skip to the next step. You don't let a good applicant get away! So, if you are joined by someone else, pull out another business card. Be professional. When the interview ends without you being hired, if the interviewer failed to produce a business card, ask for one. You want to make certain to have this person's name (with the correct spelling), and title for your next step.

Now, for your next step — You need to have a *thank you* card in your car, and before you drive away, write out the card, include another business card, and drive to the nearest post office or annex (for fast delivery), stamp it and mail it. No, not the next day, but immediately! Be professional. Now, within two days, the interviewer receives a surprise that few people manage to think about; your courteous and prompt message! Please have a thank you card in your car. I really want you to have every advantage!

If you have not heard from the company by the third working day, call the interviewer in the early afternoon. Why then? Well, you need to give your card plenty of time to get delivered. In addition, mornings are generally filled with deadlines, calls from the boss, items left over from the day before, and generally hectic. This person may likely miss lunch, or have a late one. By two or three o'clock lunch should be digesting and the calm couple of hours, if any, should be about then. Your call will best be received around two to three o'clock.

Now, you ask again for the job and hope they are happy you called!

Many companies purposely play a waiting game to see how badly the applicant wants the job. Games? No, not really.

Consider it a process of elimination, where they want the best person they can get. You at least know that this type of a hiring scenario means that this company is cautious enough to not make rash decisions and that they don't like having to go through the process any more than you do! When you get this job, you really know it's yours!

If you don't get hired, put them on your calendar for a follow-up phone call in two weeks. Why? Well, perhaps the process went a lot faster than the one we just discussed.

Let's say it all ended rather quickly and the company hired someone else. Now, two weeks later, here you are, still following up. The company already received your thank you card and a follow up call. Now two weeks later, after they realized they had hired the wrong person because he or she has been late three times, and they are not as good as they claimed and … here you are on the phone. They have a chance to immediately correct their error, and without disruption in the organization. No ads to run, no calls to make, just hand the other person a check for severance, and say goodbye to them and hello to you! This really happens often enough that I must stress the importance! Do not give up; stay in touch.

See why you never burn bridges? A rejection may hurt, but be polite whether you win or lose, and you never know what will happen. I can promise you that if you handle yourself professionally, you may lose the first round, but the next time there is an opening of any kind, you'll be hearing from them!

I'll give you another example of what a strongly confident manner can accomplish. This is another one that happened to me. I do not mean to brag, but I have only my own experience to write about here! I did not do research for this book, because it is from personal experience and I consider myself an expert. I didn't have to study other people's stories in order to teach you what I learned the hard and right way! I have had more jobs than most people, and I have interviewed multitudes of applicants.

So to my story; just to give you an idea of what can happen if you are determined and persistent! This story happened in Minnesota. I had quit my position with the Minnesota Highway Department and accepted a sales position in the southern part of the state because it seemed to have better potential. Besides that, truth be known, all future advancement in the highway department would involve more civil service tests that all had problem solving using algebra and trigonometry, which were my very worst subjects in school. I finally had passed my civil service test for technician I, after twice failing it, and I was afraid that my hatred of the exams would hold me back in the future! Maybe I was just not smart enough?

Now, here I was in southern Minnesota renting a place to live and then going to meet the sales manager. He didn't show, but he left word for me that he would be late. I panicked! In those days I barely had any money and each week was critical. Since it was early in the day, and the Minnesota Highway Department had a major field office in this city, I rushed in to make a desperate attempt at a backup plan! Since I had already rented a place, I had no choice but to get a job!

When I met the field manager of this office, he laughed! He said, "I'd love to have you, but it is absolutely impossible," he continued, "I'm so short-handed that I can't even think straight!" Then he explained a little more calmly; he said, "Son, I have five men on my list waiting in line to come to work. They have all passed their tests and are ready, but hiring has been frozen for a year. Before I could even consider you, I would first have to hire all five of them. I'm truly sorry."

Now I was even more panicky! There were no cellphones in those days, so I ran to a drug store, loaded up on change, and grabbed the nearest phone booth. You know, those glass things with the doors that you see in old movies? I started feeding the hungry phone and had the operator put me through to the headquarters of the Minnesota Highway Department in St. Paul. I asked the operator to connect me with the person in charge of hiring. I never did know how or why, but somehow I wound up speaking with the person who was the *top dog*! I don't even remember his name or title, and didn't know if he was even for real. Anyway, we must have talked a long time because I had to keep feeding the phone. Here I was, a twenty-one year old, still *wet behind the ears*, with no ability, and who just barely guessed well enough to have passed the exam, and I'm talking to the number one engineer in charge of the entire Minnesota Highway Department! I pulled out all the stops and told him my background, and really felt that we connected, but that was uncertain.

When we concluded the call, the gentleman told me to go back to the local office and he would call them. He sounded sincere and I was certainly hopeful, so I walked back around the block and entered the field office. When I walked in, the supervisor saw me from his office, and came out past his secretary, and as he approached, he said, "Gary, I'm sorry, but I told you there is no chance." I stammered, "I just spoke with Mr. Soandso (I don't remember his name) at the main office in St. Paul, and he said he was going to call you!" The man looked at me like he wanted to kick my butt out of there, shook his head and just walked back to his office. His secretary looked at me wondering if I was nuts also, and suddenly the phone rang. The look on her face was incredulous as she looked past me at her boss, and said, "Mr. Parker, its headquarters in St. Paul!" Since Mr. Parker's office was right off of the open office where I was still standing, I could visibly see his shock. He was on the phone and writing something down for several minutes, and then I heard a loud

"Thank you sir!" He got up and came out to me with his hand extended. He said, "I don't know what you did or how you did it, and I don't care, I'm so happy! I just received orders to hire all five men in line, so I can legally hire you!" I made his day, and he made mine! To this day I do not know how it happened, or what made it happen. The one thing I came away with was a gnawing and nagging feeling that I was really better at getting jobs than doing them!

Now, do you wonder how I did? Well after all that, that sales manager I mentioned returned that evening, begged me to meet him, and convinced me that he had more to offer and talked me into going to work for him instead. He sold me! So, I made another giant employment decision! I switched again, two jobs in one day!

I was so embarrassed about not taking the highway job that I wrote a letter of apology, and was so chicken I slipped the envelope through the crack in the center of their doors, and never even had the courage to drive by the office again!

There are five guys out there who likely owe me for a career. I'm hoping you enjoyed your jobs! My other job worked out, and I still can't enjoy a trigonometry problem! That, I'm sure would have been a frustrating career for me, although a secure one.

I tell you this story not to brag on me, but to show you what can be accomplished with enthusiasm and conviction. Enthusiasm is contagious! The excitement that a person can create, even in an employer, is catching. People like to hire motivators, no matter what their business is!

The next chapter was written by Wendy, and covers the best way to compete with someone who has more education than you do.

GARY and WENDY SWANSON

9 HOW TO COMPETE WITHOUT THE RIGHT EDUCATION

When you are competing with someone who has more education than you do, the first hurdle to overcome is getting an interview.

If you are asked to submit a resume before being asked to come in for an interview, you'll need to emphasize your skills and experience. I recommend that you write a *combination resume*; this type of resume begins by focusing on your skills and experience. After that you can chronologically list your previous employers. At the end, just before you list your references, you can include a section titled *Training and Education*, if you've taken any training classes or college classes.

Remember to keep your resume concise and to the point; you are not writing your life's history. In your cover letter you can briefly explain why you feel you are a good fit for the position the company is seeking to fill.

If you know the general vocation in which you want to work, sign up for a night or weekend class, or two, which is specific to your chosen field, at your local college, university or trade school. If you do this, you can put it on your resume and mention it during your interview. This will go a long way in showing your potential employer that you are very interested in improving your skills and knowledge on your own time and your own dime.

If you take the time to submit a well-written resume, and you have the necessary skills for the position, and can demonstrate that you are taking steps to improve your proficiency, there are companies that are savvy enough to see your potential and be willing to overlook your lack of formal education.

When you do get called in for an interview, do not be surprised, nor taken aback if they want to talk with you about a lower level position than you are applying for. This will very often happen when you don't have the diploma they are looking for. It just means that you are going to have to prove yourself to them, and it will take a little longer to make it to the position and pay grade you really want.

So, my advice is to set your ego and feelings aside and get your foot in the door! Continue to take more classes on your own time.

Upon my high school graduation, I received a Governor's Scholarship; it was enough to cover my tuition and books. Because it was to the university in the same town I lived in, I could have remained living with my parents and gone to school fulltime, hopefully achieving my degree in accounting.

On a work-study program, I had already been working at a small ski manufacturing company for two years in their accounting department doing accounts payable and accounts receivable duties. I enjoyed my job tremendously, from the work that I did, to the once in a while opportunity to meet famous skiers and the occasional movie actor.

When the time came to make a decision as to whether to start using my scholarship, I talked to my employer about it, and he told me that they'd like me to start work for them fulltime and if I wanted to take university classes at night, the company would pay for them. Well, needless to say, I felt flattered and very grownup; I was tired of school and wanted to move out of my parents' home and live on my own!

When the general accountant resigned, I was promoted to her position. I signed up for a few accounting classes over the next couple of years, but didn't get very far. Then, my employer decided to move his operations to another city, but I didn't want to move.

I started looking for a new place to work, and came across an ad for a manufacturing company that was just starting production who was looking for a general accountant. I sent them a resume, as they requested, and they soon called me in for an interview.

Oh my, what was I going to wear? The environment of the ski manufacturing company I worked for was very casual. In regards to dress, it had to be; the fiberglass and resin that went into making the skis found its way to every room in the building, including the offices. Standard attire, even for the office, was jeans and t-shirts. I didn't own a dress or even a pair of slacks that was suitable for an interview. I was being very careful of what I spent money on, since I didn't know how long I'd have my current job and how long it would take to find a replacement; so I didn't feel I could afford to buy a new outfit for an interview. So, I made a dress from some material I had purchased years ago for a high school sewing class project. Fortunately, it was summer, and having a tan, I was able to get away with a pair of low-heeled sandals, sans pantyhose. I do not recommend going this route, but that's for another chapter.

Afterward, I felt the interview had gone well and surely they'd offer me the job. Well, they did offer me a job, but it wasn't as the general accountant, but as the accounts payable and fixed assets clerk. I was disappointed, it was a cut in pay, but I needed a job; I had rent to pay and a car payment to make.

I accepted the position, and when I started there I found that the general accountant position was filled by another young woman my age who had just graduated from the local university with an accounting degree. I could have kicked myself! I felt I knew so much more than she did about her job. I had to teach her how to fill out debit and credit entries and how to enter them in the general ledger. I was just astonished, not to mention frustrated. I was wise enough to hold my tongue, and always treated her with respect. I was glad I did; she soon demonstrated that she was a whiz at analyzing financial statements and managing projects and people.

As the years passed, she was promoted several times and so was I. When the economy took a downturn, she was in management and was responsible for determining who got laid off. The company went through at least a half-dozen layoffs, and I heard several times through the workplace grapevine that she made sure I was never one of those unfortunate people to receive a blue slip (layoff notice).

The company recovered, and I never did catch up to her on the pay scale, but along the way I learned that I was bored with accounting and made a lateral move to the IT department as a software developer; a field that allowed me to be more creative, and one that I still love. Just think, I could have completed my schooling and achieved a degree in something I didn't want to do.

If you find a good company that you want to work for, take the position you are offered and work your way to your goal from within. Show your employer what you are capable of, work hard, and soon you will prove that a degree doesn't always equal a better employee.

GARY and WENDY SWANSON

10 RECON

When you are considering a particular company at which to apply, if you know where their employees park, it's always fun to see what they drive. Sometimes a parking lot can give you some insight into the type of people they attract.

It's always interesting to see the interaction of a company's work force, if you are able. Are they glum-faced and expressionless, or do they have an upbeat walk that exudes happiness and friendliness. Are there waves and shouts back and forth, or do they look like they are in a hurry to catch the last train from hell; or in the morning, are they late for work a lot? Normally if someone has a habit of being late, it means they don't like their job. This is true almost all of the time! Can you identify?

So, analyze you own self. Do you have a bounce in your step and show up before your shift, and oftentimes find yourself working late because you lost track of the time? If you cannot identify with this scenario, then I would suggest that you have a long talk with the person in the mirror and start looking for a better job! Besides, if you're reading this book, you likely have made this decision already.

Don't be afraid to do it; go now!

If you are one who likes to plan ahead, and the company you are considering has an employee bulletin board in their entrance, just casually go in and start reading it. If someone approaches you to offer assistance, that's a pretty good time to just admit that you are doing research because you are considering applying for a job. This works wonders sometimes, and I know people that were literally dragged in by the arm and interviewed on the spot! Sometimes it's all a matter of timing.

This is why it's always a good idea to be neatly dressed whenever you are around the company. It has happened to my clients, who just by chance, were scouting out companies, and someone has just been terminated, and by just being there, they had a chance to walk right into a job!

Incidentally, the *neatly dressed* part should always be your rule! Anytime you have reason to be on your company's property, be dressed as you would be for work! Never let your employer or fellow employees see you dressed sloppy at work. It shows disrespect for your employer and for yourself. I don't care if it is your day off!

I have a lot of friends who wear ties and jackets at work, and wear muscle t-shirts and boots, and ride Harley's on their days off; business people with loads of hidden tattoos! There have been times when I have been having coffee with a company president in his or her office when they suddenly let out an audible gasp, and as I joined them at the window, jaws agape while one of their junior executives roared through the parking lot, parked his *Hawg* in his private parking spot, got off and entered the building. You could just read the shock on their frowning faces!

Certainly we all have lives, and no one for the most part has too much concern over how each of us conducts our own business. However, once you mix the two, prepare for some consequences. I have been in these situations many times over the years, and on one specific occasion, since I was a consultant and enjoyed the executive officers' trust, I was told to, "Start looking for Marlon Brando's replacement!" Keep your private life separated from your company as a general rule.

Naturally, this applies more to the higher paying jobs, but think about that statement for a moment. Here was a hardworking, successful vice-president, who up until this day had been a well-respected member of a team! After his pronouncement, the president and I sat down, and he elaborated on his feelings. He apologized for being so crudely frank, however he went on to explain the background of his company, and how the corporate image had been carefully cultivated, and he had always maintained a policy of not interacting with his upper management socially. With the exception of two annual events that were company sponsored, the company frowned upon social involvement of its executives beyond that point. He further stated that within his circle, he would be profoundly embarrassed and possibly humiliated if he were known to have a *gangster* working for him! This was certainly a very isolated and shocking occurrence; however, it's just common sense to keep your private life to yourself. I can't even count the occasions where the company Christmas party was responsible for the downfall of so many executives.

Think about another scenario, where you tool in to your office on your day off to pick up something you forgot. Instead of driving your usual *beater* that you normally come in, today you are driving your fun car. Now what do you think your supervisor's reaction may be if he sees you hop out of your beautiful new ride that happens to be the car of his dreams? The car that due to financial difficulties he may never have a chance to own, and here you are, his junior employee, flaunting your toy! Get the picture? Exercise caution in drawing attention to yourself!

Now, back to the interview: I caution you that when you are asked if you have any questions, that you only ask the type that give you *points*! By this, I mean that you should already have enough of an idea about the position that if they told you to start tomorrow, chances are you would. So don't ask questions just for the sake of conversation. Ask about extra training opportunities that you can do at home, or if you are allowed to work later on your own time to learn more. Ask if there are courses you can take to be more knowledgeable about your job and for future advancement. Be sincere about these questions, because when you think about it, wouldn't you invest some free time for the opportunity?

Employers love to see people that are willing to invest time that they are not compensated for in order to be better at their jobs. Does this give you an idea as to why employment firms are so successful? Because they sell you better than you can sell yourself. They tell employers that their applicant wants to spend extra time studying!

If I ask you to, "Tell me about yourself." How well do you think you'll do it? I can tell you — you'll do a lousy job! You will likely stink. This is precisely why many otherwise super competent and highly skilled people will spend a huge amount of commission by having a placement firm work for them. It's a lot like consigning your used car to a dealer to sell and paying them a percentage to do it. That's why these head hunter firms are so good, because they know the questions to ask you, and they are a heck of a lot more in-depth than "Tell me about yourself!" They ask you pointed questions to draw out the *you* that lies in your subconscious. Once they have all of your good points, they put together a presentation that they can use to sell you to an employer! This is how you need to prepare yourself so that you will be able to discuss all that you have to offer.

For instance; did you ever help someone by changing their tire? Have you donated to charity? Which one, and why? Are you a veteran? What is your most vivid example of a special rescue? What pet do you remember? Just questions that often seem pointless, but when the puzzle is formed, there is a whole different you than you remembered, and would never have thought to mention, because it seemed insignificant and bragging! Believe me, it may be boring to you, but by the time the job counselor is through, you will be in line for a Nobel Prize! That's their job. Make it your job if you are representing yourself. If you won't brag on you, who will?

Now, unless you're feeling like paying a lot of money for someone to take you on consignment, sit down and get to know yourself! Have dinner or a drink together; just you and yourself. Now, write down some examples. What is your greatest accomplishment? What is your worst failure and what did you learn from it?

Write down all of your good points now; I do mean all! There is a good chance that you have forgotten many of your accomplishments in life, and maybe a thorough review of these assets need to be a part of your resume, or at least a part of your sales pitch when you are asked to tell someone about yourself! When you can sell you to me, and make me want to jump at the chance to bring you on board my company, then you will have done the proper preparation!

So you have a college degree? Okay; in many cases, that and $5 buys you a cup of coffee! Don't get me wrong; I always prefer to hire a college educated person, because they made the effort to improve themselves, and even more so if it was at their own expense! Hopefully something rubbed off. At least I know you're smart enough to pass tests! Since you have a degree, sell an employer on what you learned and how much you got out of it.

Resumes are essential, and applications are only good to get an interview, so you can use the opportunity to hand over your resume. Consider your resume as instruction to create a terrific employee, so all your employer has to do is *add water.*

I have omitted the proper preparation of resumes, because there is just tons of online advice for preparing them. I do not intend to teach you how to prepare on paper. My *job one* is to get you one job!

So many applicants send hundreds of applications and resumes every month, and there are so many computer programs that automatically apply to every job immediately after it is posted. You can be applying for jobs you don't even know about! That's super! Your computer is applying to an employer's computer, so you have two computers interviewing each other. It almost makes you unnecessary, doesn't it?

11 THE INTERVIEW

This brings me to my first days in the job market, and harkens back to my high school counselors.

They always cautioned everyone to not change jobs! Don't be a *job hopper* was the main advice people would give. I call B.S. on this, at least to a large degree! How are you going to know if you are going to like a job 'til you do it? Do people think one must stick it out no matter how bad it is to not be known as a "job hopper?" Well call me Jiminy Cricket because I have had more jobs than you could imagine!

Changing jobs is really not all that much of a concern to an employer if there is logic to the progression. If it shows an advancement each time, it shows the possibility that the applicant has a record of constant improvement. One may assume that this person is a fast learner, and indicate that they expect to be promoted when they qualify. More cautious employers may have a problem with hiring this individual if they know they will never have an opportunity for advancement to offer them. This situation may be best for applicant and employer!

When you do get the interview, be sure to bring a proper resume! Even if they do not ask for it, bring it along. Do not ever try to substitute your resume for their application however; as you need to show them you can follow directions.

I have had people hand me their resume and say, "Why don't I give you this instead?" And I always think, "Why you impertinent S.O.B., fill the damned thing out!" What I actually say is, "I'll take that, thank you, but I really need both." You won't control me when I'm interviewing you!

When in the interview, be observant! Most people in any position of authority display the things, in their offices, of which they are the most proud! Before you start gushing for the things displayed, first ascertain that this is actually the interviewer's office! It may just be an all purposes office for conferences and interviews.

It would be most embarrassing to blurt out, "Oh, I see you are a Lakers fan; me too," and have the interviewer look up startled and says, "No, I'm from Portland, and the Lakers are my least favorite team. I think the Blazers are the best in the world!"

Little late to regroup now, isn't it? Observe your interviewer carefully. Is he or she egotistical? Are they sporting a Rolex, or worse yet, a Rolex knock off? One way or another, this person wants to be complimented! Just don't say, "Oh, that's a nice watch, is it real?" If it is a fake, they will be embarrassed and feel you could tell, and if it's real, they will dislike you for being so rude as to think they are the type of person to be phony! "Nice watch" is enough said!

Is the gentleman across from you wearing a masonic ring? I always wear mine, because it has always been a sign to other

Freemasons that I am a brother; and to non-masons, as a sign that I can be trusted.

Lapel pins are always an indication of an affiliation, and it never hurts to inquire about one that you don't recognize, and to acknowledge those with which you are familiar.

People adorn themselves with treasures and mementos that they are proud of, and a polite inquiry is never out of line, and oftentimes will lead to a pleasant conversation and a better interview.

Because of your advance research, look for the right opportunity to stress that reason you selected as to why you would like to work for this company. Don't be phony, but you can always look for some reason that will stir pride in the interviewer. Don't forget that if you recognize the fact and state it aloud, why you respect this company, you reinforce the fact that the interviewer must also be very proud to be an employee as well. Nothing phony, but as I said, you can always find something about anyone or any company that stands out as something to be proud of.

Even if they are not all that happy with their job, if you show a respect for their position and for their company, you will score points! You respect their employer and you respect their personal importance, and they will in turn, like you and hire you, if for nothing more than the fact that you look up to them!

Sounds nuts, I know, but it ain't rocket science! It's human nature. How can you not like someone who pays you a sincere compliment? Be careful though, because bullshit flows downhill!

Looking back on my experiences as an employment counselor, I know for a fact that the majority of people are not all that happy with their jobs! The majority of people feel unappreciated by their employers. Some of this stems from the ignorance of employers who feel that if they praise their people too much on their performance, then they may be expectant of pay increases. The old keep 'em guessing philosophy is a poor way to run a railroad, but so many companies do.

This high percentage of seemingly unappreciated people who may be conducting these interviews, works to the advantage of the job applicant! Tread cautiously in this area, because if you play your role correctly, you may just end up with a new and rewarding job.

Realizing human nature, you are now very well prepared for your interview, and if you now use this knowledge, you may start your new job soon! Now, whatever happens, keep it to yourself! Never, ever brag to anyone about how you sucked up to the interviewer and had him or her eating out of your hand! Don't betray what I am giving you; any more than you would your daddy's secret fishing hole!

It's not necessary to talk disrespectfully about someone who you are able to control and manipulate! It's just not cool!

It sounds like a strange way to get a job, but when you think about it, it's all just human nature! The legendary Will Rogers said, "I never met a man I didn't like." They say that he most likely meant that he could certainly find something to like in everyone! I can think of some acquaintances that would take a bit more searching to find something I like, but it makes sense.

So, your objective on the interview is obviously to get hired. The more it pays, the harder it will be to get, right? You may very well have to go through several interviews at different levels of management. This is understandable, as the company has these cautionary procedures to minimize their likelihood of making a poor decision. Hiring, training and merging in a new employee can be a very difficult process. If they make a mistake, it can be very costly in morale and production.

Junior level management will take the first run at the interviews. Getting by the first ones can be fairly easy for experienced applicants, but one must be cautious, as sometimes these people will have enough authority to prevent certain applicants from proceeding to the next level. If they should perceive you to be someone who would soon challenge their own job, they will try their best to eliminate you on the first round. Just be polite and courteous, even though your skill level may be very obvious to be much greater than the person conducting the interview; there may be a well thought out reason for this. Perhaps a test to see how you handle subordinates.

Some companies have a lot of psychological tests that they put an applicant through. Some companies even go to the extreme of having their applicants talk to a psychologist to make sure you will be a good fit for the company. Their reasoning behind this is usually because they don't want to waste time, effort and money on someone who is not going to stay with them for a good, long while. They feel by having the applicant talk to a psychologist, who is familiar with the workings of the company, they'll find out whether the person will get along well with their long-term employees, and in the case of a high-pressure job, how well the person can handle stress and deadlines.

Some of the biggest surprises I've had over the years were when I thought the test to be such a ridiculous mess of confusion, and then when I had record high scores, I had a new respect for them! Ha-ha!

Make certain to never criticize any of your previous employers, as people are leery of hiring someone with grudges, and who talk about their last bosses, because they feel you someday may turn on them as well.

No matter how you feel about your last company, never betray any confidences, operating procedures, or just anything about their operations.

Try to answer any questions regarding your previous employer as if your old boss was sitting in on your interview. Always be respectful, no matter why you left! You can say you are looking for a new job to advance your career, or to learn new skills, but never imply your previous employer was holding you back.

One thing you must always remember; chisel it in stone and carry it with you, so you never forget…**Always**, be certain to *ask for the job!*

I remember back to my employment counselor days. I had sent an applicant on his fourth interview with the same company. After each of the first three interviews, the employer asked to see my client again. For reasons I took to be uncertainty and caution, I just kept sending my client back, and after each interview we talked, and he was enthusiastic about how the interview went, figuring that they were just slow in deciding. After the fourth interview, I called the owner of the company and asked what was going on? I said "My client is perfect for your company! What gives?" The gentleman said, "I know that! I really wanted to hire him too, that's why I kept bringing him back!" So, I asked what the problem was. He sighted deeply and said, "Joe (remember I'm Joe Lee), I will not ever hire anyone who doesn't want the job enough to ask for it! I've had this man back four times hoping he would just ask for the job and he never did!

Today was his last chance; find me someone else." Big lesson!

Always ask for the job. When you come to the point in conversation where the interviewer asks if you have any questions, your answer could be, "How soon may I start?" Play it by ear. You don't want to appear too cocky, but confidence has a way of appearing that way! I have asked questions like, "Where is the employee parking?"

Just make sure to let them know that you want the job, and don't ask too many *benefits* questions! This applies especially to sales positions! An employer who is hiring salespeople does not react well to the applicant asking questions on hours, insurance, and other security conscious type questions. They are looking for salespeople who have confidence in their ability to earn a good living, and the benefits questions indicate fear and weakness. This can be true of many positions, not just sales!

Asking a sales manager about the hours you are expected to work will often draw an answer such as, "You'll be on the 'B' schedule." When you ask what the 'B' schedule is; he or she answers, "Be here!"

The sales industry wants self-confident and aggressive people who are sure of themselves and their ability to earn a good living; enough so that they can buy their own benefits!

If you are interviewing for a position where you will be working for the person who is doing the interview, you need to walk a fine line until you ascertain what he or she is looking for.

Being aggressive is certainly a desirable quality, and a lot of applicants think they will be most impressive if they boldly state the old, "I want your job!" approach.

This will work in the situation where you could have an effect over getting this person promoted to the next level, and you then would move up into theirs.

What happens though in the case where your interviewer has reached his or her maximum level of competency with this company? They have tried repeatedly for promotions and have been turned down on each occasion. They are sidelined, and they know it. You may have just skated onto thin ice! Maybe also, the reason that they have the opening is because the last person who had the job you are applying for started making runs for a promotion, and your interviewer managed to find a way to get rid of the person in order to protect their own position. Now you come along and without realizing it, become a threat to your interviewer.

This type of boldness and brashness is best saved for an interview with this person's boss. Companies thrive by *dangling the carrot*, so just save your desires to achieve for the proper level of management.

When you do run into a situation where you sense that you have much more ability than the one sitting across from you, just focus on the job being offered, and refrain from showing your aggression until you have something to gain!

If you are in a multi-phase interview process, just make certain to get to the next interview. Use enough of your ammo to get to the next step, and save the dynamite for the next performance.

Now, there will come a time when you know you want the job, and you are certain that you have but one chance at it, so throw out all the stops and go for broke!

I'll give you an example that I used when I was confronted with the *opportunity of a lifetime*! I was working for a loan company in Madison, Wisconsin and had just returned from another city after relieving the manager of another branch while he took a much needed vacation. As a relief manager, I was next in line for my own office. Even though it was a good job, it still did not carry the prestige that working for a bank did, and periodically, I checked the newspaper ads.

Being tired from a week in another city, it was late in the evening before I checked the ads. There, in a bold ad, was the job I had not even known existed! It was a large and detailed ad. The Bank of Madison and its' branch in Hillsdale, Wisconsin were looking for someone for their loan department. Their loan portfolio for their automobile and R.V. loans were under supervision of a firm of banking experts out of New Jersey and was rapidly expanding. The bank was directly across from the state Capitol, and I wanted this job bad!

The bank was closed, so I had to wait until Monday, and when I called first thing in the morning, I was told that the supervisor was at their branch bank that morning; so I just jumped in my car and sped to the branch!

When I entered this beautiful new building, I was immediately impressed with the plush carpets, mahogany desks and giant leather chairs. The Safari Club couldn't have been more imposing! I just knew that *I had arrived*!

Upon being greeted by a receptionist, I explained my reason for being there; she explained that she was "sure the job had been filled," but she called the man in charge for me, and shortly I was introduced to an immaculately dressed gentleman who led me to his oversized desk, looking out the huge windows at the beautiful new landscaping. As I sank into the leather chair, my heart sank even deeper as he told me I was three days too late!

He expressed a desire to discuss the position, and said he would like to retain my file for future opportunities they may have, and the more he explained the job, the more I wanted it! He said that he had hired another man on Friday and he was already 90% completed with his paperwork. He was due to start work the next week.

Now, picture this beautiful desk sitting with four others stretched across the splendid floors in front of twenty foot high windows looking out on the golf course type landscaping; the tellers windows stretched down the long, open corridor about twenty feet away from the desks. This was truly a magnificent and prestigious operation, and I wanted in!

The more we talked, the more we both realized that I would have been perfect for this job, but he had interviewed over 35 people last week, and it was done. He said that I would be given the very next opening in any of their branches in the United States. That did not heal my wounds however, and I suddenly did one of the craziest things I had ever done! I figured I had nothing to lose.

I jumped up, leaned over the center of his desk, and slammed my fist down so hard that his pen set actually hopped up in the air! I very loudly and forcefully stated, "Mr. Childers, I want this job!"

He shot out of his chair, rising to his full height, towering over me by over a foot, and I thought he might hit me, as his face was red; and just as loudly he proclaimed, "You've got it! Anyone who wants the job that bad, I have to hire." He then reached out and pumped my hand.

Sitting back down, we were both visibly charged, and he said, "I just couldn't let you get away! I'll find something else for the other fellow to do."

It turned out to be a fantastic job, even better than I had imagined! Looking back on that experience, I can truthfully say, "It was a magnificent performance," because it was spontaneous and honest! I was mad to see that I had just seen the ideal job slip away, and I was going to go get it and bring it back!

To further explain, in case anyone does not understand what happened; I really lost control of my professional demeanor, and demonstrated my disappointment forcefully, and although it was impetuous, I was also acting, because I had nothing to lose! Had I not taken that job, my decision to work for a bank had been made, and I would have just gone for another one!

This may never happen to you, but keep this example in mind, because if the opportunity ever presents itself, "What do you have to lose?" Sure I had been grandstanding, but I was sincere, and I had to have that job!

You are going to succeed in life; I promise you! Why? Because you're reading this book, and I have been incredibly successful, and I'm here to help you! Why? To sell books? Certainly, but the honest reason is because my ego is so damned big, I want to be able to take credit for the successful careers of thousands of people! Fair enough?

A final note and a caution on being complimentary to your interviewer. They are not stupid, so keep the flowery comments out of your discussion.

They have maybe just purchased that beautiful pair of Taryn Rose shoes, and they only wore them today because they are attending a special party right after work. Here you are saying, "Oh, I love your Taryn Rose shoes, I have six pair and really enjoy them!" This person perhaps saved for months to cough up the four hundred clams for those shoes, and you have six pair! Maybe you *don't need* this job; at least in her mind!

Things on the wall or desk are great to notice; they want you to (make sure it is their office you're sitting in). Just leave the personal compliments to the next person who won't be hired.

If you are applying for a higher level position, there is normally a process of elimination; first you are screened by a more junior employee, and then up to the next level, so let's not count on hitting one out of the park. Let's just concentrate on getting on base! Just like a golf game, we take it one hole at a time and each leg is different.

Dress your best and be professional. Don't answer questions with yeah, nope, uh-huh, or any other grammatical absurdities. If I run a western store, don't apply to me by saying, "Howdy!" You can *howdy* my customers, but it's "How do you do sir?" to me. If your interviewer is Latino, don't get cute with a, "Buenos dias" to her or otherwise show your *inbred lack of intelligence*. Just use a higher level of common sense!

You're probably shaking your head saying, "Now who would be so stupid?" I can answer that easily; the person who just interviewed ahead of you who was a lot more qualified than you. He just acted *way to cocky*, so congratulations, *you're hired*!

Now you can hand over your resume and hope they take the time to read it. If not, then be glad that you had the eyeball to eyeball session where you had a chance to show your enthusiasm! Please remember this. That is the reason that I put so much emphasis on it!

There will be those inexperienced or nervous interviewers that may ask for your resume up front, and many companies will insist on it. These situations will logically be used more often for the type of positions that require more technical skills than personality. Just play it by ear and roll with the punches.

A few additional tips: Avoid controversial lapel pins. The American flag is always a plus. Belts and shoes much match, and shoes must be shined!

Refrain from using that shot of mouth spray, as the alcohol in it will linger long enough to make your interviewer wonder if you've been drinking. Mints like Tic Tacs are safe.

I must mention here that I have carried Tic Tacs for years, but not the rattley plastic box that sounds like a loud baby rattle when you reach for one. I put a few in a shirt pocket for quick and easy access. After having a cup of coffee with a prospective employer and the next higher up may suddenly want you to come into his or her office for further discussion, you may casually slip in to your pocket for a mint to kill your dragon breath!

You may find yourself being interviewed by the owner's son whose nose you flattened in school, or the class nerd whose parents are trying to bring him along in the family business. Just be even more polite, no matter how you may resent doing it! Just like the military has always instructed; *salute the rank, not the person.* Think of how far you may get if after eight years of contempt for this kid who's now your chance for a job if you say, "Yes sir, thank you sir." Even if your sincerity may be in doubt, his ego will make him believe you. It's human nature, and it works every time! You just need to *fake it till you make it!*

I'm certain that you have already noticed how many of the *good jobs* are filled from within. Right? So how do we compete with that fact?

Think about this; many job seekers are allowing pride to hold them back from using common sense. If you're unemployed now and going through the frustrations of the long dry spell; it only gets worse. To get promoted from within, you must first be *within!* Instead of continually being turned down by applying for jobs you're qualified for, consider applying for those jobs you are over qualified for!

Just consider the fact before you total go bananas by saying, "I can't take a step backwards!" Why not? What if you did? Who would laugh at you? Certainly no one in the company you apply to. They'd love to have you, right? Also consider this; how easy would your new job be, and how impressive would you look to those in upper management? Don't most people usually go for jobs at the level that challenges them more and has trials and failures? So you go in and absolutely ace this job! No mistakes, just excellent performance right out of the gate!

What do you think happens if someone at the next level above you *stubs their toe?* Here comes the promotion from within, and since you have a perfect record, congratulations on your promotion! This especially holds true of the better companies whose policy is to always try to promote from within so they build that tremendous loyalty!

I know it's not easy to partially start over, but maybe you should consider that maybe you're not as good as you think you are. No insult intended, but don't we all go through this self-analysis when we are out of a job? Of course we do; so think hard about your abilities and your previous employer. How hard was it to get that last job? Why did you lose it, or if you're still employed and contemplating a change, how hard was it to get hired where you now work?

Perhaps the title and pay grade for the new company is less prestigious than the one you now hold, but just maybe there is more responsibility connected with that position than you now have. It might be worth considering why those jobs are so much harder to get. Maybe the income is the same even though the title may not be.

Could it be that the reason that firm is so desirous to work at is because its' people are so valuable to them and treated so well is the very fact that they are more proficient at every level? That means that when they promote from within, the person receiving the promotion is very well qualified for it and is assured a successful transition.

It may just be worth it to swallow your pride and think about your future years! Just consider it like going on a long hike to get to a remote and beautiful place on the ocean shore. Where the beauty is pristine and unsurpassed! You will likely have hills, maybe mountains and valleys, but going up and down until you reach your destination is part of life!

Never consider it a failure to drop back down to a lesser job, as long as it is a part of your ultimate goal; which is a successful career! Who ever really knows when they are under 25 years of age what they really want out of life? Who ever really knows when they're 50? Sure, they can all tell you what they wish they'd have done, but if truth be known, most of us never really go straight through life on the same track we planned early in life! How can an inexperienced mind, with nothing other than advice from people that tell them what they wish they had done with their lives, ever formulate a lifetime goal?

So never be concerned about changing jobs or careers. It's your life! To quote Kirk Douglas in his personal favorite movie, *Lonely Are the Brave*, "Do what you want to do, and to hell with everybody else!" It's harsh to say, but really; you only go around once, so who do you need to impress and satisfy but you? It goes without saying that family concerns need to be considered, but working at the *wrong* job will do more to harm your family than anything else. Just don't be like Cousin Eddie in Chevy Chase's *Christmas Vacation*, and have nine years of unemployment while *holding out for a management job*! Pay your dues.

Is there no one out there who isn't afraid to speak up? To try do something different; to think outside the proverbial job box?

Who established the rules? Well, doesn't it seem like employers did? So everyone that hopes to get a job by conforming to what the big bosses surmise to be the ideal candidate? They want everyone to look the same and perform like robots; right? Okay, that is fine, once I'm hired! I won't object to looking like all the other *toy soldiers* coming off the assembly line, but how do I get noticed enough up front?

Sometimes one has to just take a chance! So how do we be different enough to be noticed, but the same enough to want them to hire us? Well, you heard me pound my fist on the banker's desk! I don't know if I'd do that again, but the look of shock on his face and the results were certainly worth it! I guess if you look at it as if you have nothing to lose; why not!

Okay, so what do you have to lose? You don't have the job now, and you may not be likely to get it by just filling out the application and going through the routine. If you don't have anything but a remote chance, then that's all you stand to lose. On the other hand, if you stand out enough, you just may get a shot!

Once I sent out a letter to an employer that simply said, "You will be receiving a very large package in three days! Please treat it with care, because it will be me! I am coming to see you about a job with your company." I really enjoyed our first face to face meeting, and the job and pay I received while working for them!

Showing up at the same company every day and asking for an interview will possibly get you barred from the place, but more than likely, someone at a management level will certainly come out, if for no other reason than to find out if you're insane. What may really happen is that you well get undivided time with management to explain why you are being so persistent on working for them when they don't even have an opening. Now do what you came for — Interview! Sell yourself!

Sound crazy? Yes. Just crazy enough to work three times out of seven! That's better odds than you get by dropping off applications.

Oh, did I mention *never be late?* If I didn't, then we'd better discuss it now! If you show up late for an interview, you don't deserve the job! Live your life by this fact — Successful people are never late!

How many alarm clocks do you set each day? You probably answered one, right? Wrong! Buy another one. Every night you set two clocks. The main one needs to work off of electricity, but it must have a 9-volt or similar battery backup. Change the battery when you change batteries in your smoke alarm so they are always fresh. Now buy a battery only alarm, and when you set it, set the wake up time for ten minutes later than the main clock. This way you will never be late!

No, traffic doesn't count, flat tires don't count! Plan your trip to work, or an interview, by allowing an extra half hour to 45 minutes extra drive time; double that if you live in a larger city or use public transportation. If that sounds like a huge waste to you, then I'd say you'd better start looking for a better job than you are presently considering by reading this book! Why? Because obviously the job you want to get is not important enough to *never be late for*!

I learned this lesson long, long ago while working at a job I hated, but it was a paycheck. One day the foreman, who was a super-nice guy, just mentioned, "Gary, I notice that you're usually about five or ten minutes late for work. Now I don't care myself, because I'm a lifer with this company, but normally people who are late quite a bit are unhappy with their job." I thought about it for a couple of days, and you know, he was right. I had never thought about it! Three days later I resigned, found a job that was fun and was never late again; in over 40 years with any employer! Reason being was twofold; I learned that I was unhappy, and I never again took a job I didn't like!

Never be late! Especially never on your interview day! Make a dry run before that day. Know where to park and how long in traffic it will take to get there. On interview day, you'd better allow enough time to be there 15 minutes to ½ hour early! Even if you have to sit in your car!

I would highly suggest that you take care of the two alarm setup immediately!

The only time you should ever be referenced to as being late should be on your *epitaph*, and if you're late for your new job, start chiseling your name!

12 ANOTHER OPTION

Here's where you need to keep an open mind; so open your mental doors and windows and just think about this. While you're in limbo, waiting for something to come open so you can at least make a living as you continue to pursue the job you hope to eventually land, why not consider sales?

I heard that! You say, "Oh, I could never do that! I could never push people into buying something they don't want. I'm just not that type of person!" Okay, now that you got that off your chest, why not listen for a bit?

First of all, people do not get pushed into buying something they don't want! They want it, or they wouldn't look at it. A person cannot be talked into buying something stupid! They can be talked into paying stupid amounts of money perhaps, but they wouldn't buy it if they didn't want it! Remember that.

This may be a good solution for you to make some good money while you wait and continue to hand out resumes.

I know huge numbers of people who also thought they could never sell anything, but they took a sales position to feed their families while they waited, and would up staying and making a great career out of it.

If you are unemployed or just barely getting by while hoping to find a new career, how would you feel about selling cars for a living? Disgusting thought, right? Now what if I told you that the average automobile salesperson earns between $3,000 per month on the lower end and up to an average of $5,000 to $8,000 at the mid-level, and with the cream of the crop earning around 10 to 12 thousand dollars every month? I know this for a fact, as once I stopped bouncing around the country and realized where the money was, I spent 30 years in management in the retail automobile business!

Yes, that's me; I realize you are not like that, but here you are, out there trying to sell yourself and you see how difficult it is, but why not consider some type of sales while you wait? If you're after a job that will pay you $4,000 a month, would you suffer with $5,000 a month while you wait!

Please don't sell yourself short by saying you couldn't do it. Maybe you're right, but I would like to challenge that *stinkin' thinkin'* and ask you to look into it. What do you have to lose?

I have a book on the market titled "Car Sharks and Closers" which is a complete training manual for the automobile business. It teaches salespeople, sales managers, finance managers and dealers the entire sales process. I teach the exact verbiage to use in selling, and the psychology of the car deal from the initial greeting through exact negotiation strategies and closes that work wonders!

If you are considering a sales career, many other professionals are utilizing the techniques in my book; from real estate to door-to-door sales!

As a healthy alternative, give sales a try. You may decide to never leave it once you see what kind of money can be made.

Companies with products to sell are always looking for more talent; yes, they have turnover, because twenty percent of people can't sell. That's accurate! There is turnover because good salespeople have a tendency to often pursue new opportunities, and when you're good at selling, you can pretty much write your own ticket.

Early in life, I heard a world renowned speaker say, "Nothing happens in the world until somebody sells something!" Think about that statement. Could we even survive without selling? I don't think so. People sell food, gas, clothing, cars, equipment, homes, furniture, education; just about everything you own, use or see has been sold by someone at some time! Yes, even the clean water in your faucet, your grass seed, your trees in your yard, everything in your home and office. Most everything we depend on for our survival and enjoyment must be sold by someone to someone else!

Certainly the Native Americans were not as dependent as we are today, but they bartered as far back as recorded time; which is the purest form of sales.

Many years ago when Boeing in Seattle had a major strike, their people were locked out. Now what does a highly paid engineer do when he or she has a family to feed? I can tell you truly that I never have seen so many over-qualified people with master's degrees applying for jobs selling cars! There were countless people applying for these positions to me, and this was when I was in Portland, Oregon. These applicants were three hours away from home and wanting to sell cars.

Why do you suppose they chose that field? Could it be because they were more outgoing than other people?

Engineers? Are you kidding me? No! Engineers are not the type of people that you normally consider to be the outgoing, flashy, loud and brash image of the typical car salesperson! They were applying to sell cars because they were smart enough to know that's where the money was!

It wasn't necessary to change their personalities, because the image is a false one. Any person with a neat appearance, and a good personality that can carry on a decent conversation, can be taught to sell. It's not all smoke and mirrors, but it does require one to know all about what they are selling. Lying is not part of the criteria, and you won't last long if you do.

Do not confuse the high paying jobs with the salaried sales positions. In order to make the big bucks, you must have at least part of your pay based on your individual performance. The more you sell, the more you make!

I would caution against attempting careers such as real estate sales that require a lot of study and the checks are slow in coming, unless you have the bankroll to last until you learn the ropes. If you do, it is a great career, and is one that I am currently doing.

Anyway, you can see why I'm passionate about selling, because it's a career that never gets dull or stale, and as I mentioned before; *you can write your own ticket,* and believe me I have!